DATE DUE

Biography Today

Profiles of People of Interest to Young Readers

Sports Series

Volume 4

Laurie Lanzen Harris
Executive Editor

Cherie D. Abbey
Co-Editor

615 Griswold Street • Detroit, Michigan 48226

Laurie Lanzen Harris, *Executive Editor*
Cherie D. Abbey, *Co-Editor*
Kevin Hillstrom and Laurie Hillstrom, *Sketch Writers*
Joan Margeson and Barry Puckett, *Research Associates*

Omnigraphics, Inc.

* * *

Peter E. Ruffner, *Senior Vice President*
Matthew P. Barbour, *Vice President — Operations*
Laurie Lanzen Harris, *Vice President — Editorial*
Thomas J. Murphy, *Vice President — Finance*
Jane J. Steele, *Marketing Coordinator*
Kevin Hayes, *Production Coordinator*

* * *

Frederick G. Ruffner, Jr., Publisher

Contents

Preface

Welcome to the fourth volume of the **Biography Today Sports Series**. We are publishing this series in response to the growing number of suggestions from our readers, who want more coverage of more people in *Biography Today*. Several volumes, covering **Artists, Authors, Scientists and Inventors, Sports Figures, and World Leaders,** have appeared thus far in the Subject Series. Each of these hardcover volumes is 200 pages in length and covers approximately 12 individuals of interest to readers ages 9 and above. The length and format of the entries will be like those found in the regular issues of *Biography Today*, but there is **no duplication** between the regular series and the special subject volumes.

The Plan of the Work

As with the regular issues of *Biography Today*, this special subject volume on **Sports** was especially created to appeal to young readers in a format they can enjoy reading and readily understand. Each volume contains alphabetically arranged sketches. Each entry provides at least one picture of the individual profiled, and bold-faced rubrics lead the reader to information on birth, youth, early memories, education, first jobs, marriage and family, career highlights, memorable experiences, hobbies, and honors and awards. Each of the entries ends with a list of easily accessible sources designed to lead the student to further reading on the individual and a current address. Obituary entries are also included, written to provide a perspective on the individual's entire career. Obituaries are clearly marked in both the table of contents and at the beginning of the entry.

Biographies are prepared by Omnigraphics editors after extensive research, utilizing the most current materials available. Those sources that are generally available to students appear in the list of further reading at the end of the sketch.

Indexes

Beginning with all publications in 1999, a new Index appeared in *Biography Today*. In an effort to make the index easier to use, we have combined the **Name** and **General Index** into one, called the **General Index**. This new index contains the names of all individuals who have appeared in *Biography Today* since the series began. The names appear in bold faced type, followed by the issue in which they appeared. The General Index also contains the occupations and ethnic and minority origins of individuals profiled. The General Index is cumulative, including references to all individuals who have appeared in the *Biography Today* General Series and the *Biography Today* Special Subject volumes since the series began in 1992.

The Birthday Index and Places of Birth Index will continue to appear in all Special Subject volumes.

Our Advisors

This volume was reviewed by an Advisory Board comprised of librarians, children's literature specialists, and reading instructors so that we could make sure that the concept of this publication — to provide a readable and accessible biographical magazine for young readers — was on target. They evaluated the title as it developed, and their suggestions have proved invaluable. Any errors, however, are ours alone. We'd like to list the Advisory Board members, and to thank them for their efforts.

Sandra Arden, *Retired*
Assistant Director
Troy Public Library, Troy, MI

Gail Beaver
Ann Arbor Huron High School Library
and the University of Michigan School
of Information and Library Studies
Ann Arbor, MI

Marilyn Bethel
Pompano Beach Branch Library
Pompano Beach, FL

Eileen Butterfield
Waterford Public Library
Waterford, CT

Linda Carpino
Detroit Public Library
Detroit, MI

Helen Gregory
Grosse Pointe Public Library
Grosse Pointe, MI

Jane Klasing, *Retired*
School Board of Broward County
Fort Lauderdale, FL

Marlene Lee
Broward County Public Library System
Fort Lauderdale, FL

Judy Liskov
Waterford Public Library
Waterford, CT

Sylvia Mavrogenes
Miami-Dade Public Library System
Miami, FL

Carole J. McCollough
Wayne State University School of
Library Science, Detroit, MI

Deborah Rutter
Russell Library, Middletown, CT

Barbara Sawyer
Groton Public Library and Information
Center, Groton, CT

Renee Schwartz
School Board of Broward County
Fort Lauderdale, FL

Lee Sprince
Broward West Regional Library
Fort Lauderdale, FL

Susan Stewart, *Retired*
Birney Middle School Reading
Laboratory, Southfield, MI

Ethel Stoloff, *Retired*
Birney Middle School Library
Southfield, MI

Our Advisory Board stressed to us that we should not shy away from controversial or unconventional people in our profiles, and we have tried to follow their advice. The Advisory Board also mentioned that the sketches might be useful in reluctant reader and adult literacy programs, and we would value any comments librarians might have about the suitability of our magazine for those purposes.

Your Comments Are Welcome

Our goal is to be accurate and up-to-date, to give young readers information they can learn from and enjoy. Now we want to know what you think. Take a look at this issue of *Biography Today*, on approval. Write or call me with your comments. We want to provide an excellent source of biographical information for young people. Let us know how you think we're doing.

Laurie Harris
Executive Editor, *Biography Today*
Omnigraphics, Inc.
615 Griswold Street
Detroit, MI 48226
Fax: 1-800-875-1340

Wilt Chamberlain 1936-1999

American Professional Basketball Player
Scored an NBA Record 100 Points in a Single Game
in 1962

BIRTH

Wilton Norman Chamberlain was born on August 21, 1936, in Philadelphia, Pennsylvania. He was one of 11 children (only nine of whom survived to adulthood) born to William Chamberlain, who worked as a welder in a shipyard and as a janitor and handyman, and Olivia Chamberlain, who worked as a maid.

YOUTH

Chamberlain was raised in a mostly black, working-class neighborhood in Philadelphia. Although his family was never wealthy, they always had the things they really needed. "My folks managed. They didn't deny us anything that mattered," Wilt recalled. "We always had clothes on our backs and food on the table." Since they lived in a modest, four-bedroom house, the nine Chamberlain children did not get much privacy growing up. "We doubled up on sleeping," he noted. "We even slept four in a bed when the girls were younger."

The Chamberlain children were all expected to pitch in by doing chores around the house and working at part-time jobs after school and on weekends. Some of Wilt's earliest jobs included washing windows, shoveling snow, cleaning basements, and carrying groceries for neighbors. Later on, he started collecting valuable materials from other people's trash and selling them to local junkyards. He claimed that these early work experiences helped him later in life: "Jobs taught me the value of a dollar and the value of my own work."

From a very early age, it was clear that Chamberlain was going to be extremely tall. Surprisingly, both of his parents were under five feet, ten inches tall, and the tallest of his siblings was six feet, five inches tall. But Wilt had already reached six feet, three inches by the time he finished elementary school, and he eventually grew to be over seven feet, one inch tall. His height sometimes created problems when he was a boy. "I'd go to the movies with my family and friends. They'd get in for children's prices. I had to pay adult prices, which you didn't have to pay until you were 11," he remembered. "The woman in the booth thought I had to be older because I was so tall." Chamberlain's childhood nickname was "Dip" or "Big Dipper," because he always had to dip down to pass through doorways.

EDUCATION

Despite his gangly appearance, Chamberlain was always very well-coordinated. He played a wide variety of sports as a kid, but his favorite was track and field. His long strides made him a great runner in the 440- and 880-yard events, and he also excelled in the high jump and shot put. The one game he rarely played was basketball. "I always thought it was a sissy game," he recalled. "It wasn't like running or football. I just didn't have

Chamberlain as a 17-year-old high school senior

any desire to play." Finally, in junior high school, Chamberlain agreed to try out for the basketball team to get people to stop bothering him about it. He ended up enjoying himself, and from that time on he spent all his spare time practicing basketball. In 1951, he led his YMCA team to victory in a national tournament against much older boys. As a result, scouts for college and professional basketball teams began watching him before he even entered high school.

At Overbrook High School in Philadelphia, Chamberlain and his four closest friends made up the starting five on the varsity basketball team. During Chamberlain's three years there, the school posted a record of 58-3 and won two Philadelphia city championships. Chamberlain scored 50 points per game on a regular basis. In his senior season, over 200 recruiters attended his games. In fact, recruiters called and visited his home so often that his high school coach had to step in and supervise their contact with his family. Shortly after his graduation in 1955, Chamberlain was selected in the NBA draft by the Philadelphia Warriors—even though he would not be eligible to play in the NBA for four more years (at that time, the NBA rules did not allow players to join the league straight out of high school).

CAREER HIGHLIGHTS

College—Kansas Jayhawks

Of all the options open to him, Chamberlain eventually chose to attend Kansas University (KU) in Lawrence, Kansas. Although the school was not a basketball powerhouse at that time, going there would give him an opportunity to play for legendary coach Phog Allen. Unfortunately, Chamberlain was met with racism on his first day on the KU campus. When he went to a local restaurant for dinner, the owner refused to serve him because he was black. At first he wanted to turn around and go back to Philadelphia, but instead he informed his coach that he would not accept discrimination. The coach talked to a number of local business owners and warned them that KU's star basketball player would leave town if they continued to have a policy of segregation. Over the next few years, Chamberlain made a point of visiting nearly every restaurant in town and never again experienced a problem.

Chamberlain continued to impress people with his talents on the basketball court at KU. School rules required him to play on the freshman squad his first year, and he helped them earn an easy victory over every team they played—including the KU varsity. Upon joining the varsity in his sophomore year, Chamberlain scored 52 points and grabbed 31 rebounds in his very first game. The Jayhawks posted an impressive 21-2 record that season and won the Big Eight championship. Their success continued in the NCAA championship tournament, as they advanced all the way to the finals.

In the national championship game, the Jayhawks faced the powerful University of North Carolina Tarheels. Their opponents' entire game plan was focused upon stopping Chamberlain. First, as the Jayhawks brought the ball down the court, the Tarheels' center would try to deny him the ball. Then, when Chamberlain did receive a pass, three Tarheels players would immediately move between him and the basket. Chamberlain still managed to score 23 points and was named the tournament's most valuable player, but KU lost the championship game 54-53 in triple overtime.

Chamberlain returned to KU for his junior year in 1957. He averaged 30 points per game and was named an All-American for the second time that year, but the Jayhawks did not fare as well in the NCAA tournament. By this time, Coach Allen had retired and Chamberlain had become increasingly frustrated with the punishment he took from opposing defense players on the court. So he made the decision to leave Kansas after his junior year without earning a degree.

Harlem Globetrotters

Since Chamberlain was not allowed to play in the NBA for another year — when his class graduated from college — he jumped at the chance to play professional basketball with the famous Harlem Globetrotters during the 1958 season. The Globetrotters traveled all over the world playing exhibitions against professional teams. They had helped popularize the game of basketball with their combination of skilled play and entertaining comedy bits. Chamberlain viewed his year with the Globetrotters as an opportunity to see the world and improve his skills as well as to earn some money by playing basketball: he signed a contract for $65,000 and used the money to buy his parents a new house. In fact, he often got to prove that he could handle the ball by playing guard for the Globetrotters. Although he left the team at the end of the season to join the NBA, he would rejoin them every summer for the next 12 years.

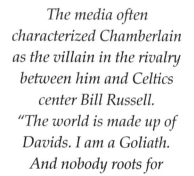

The media often characterized Chamberlain as the villain in the rivalry between him and Celtics center Bill Russell. "The world is made up of Davids. I am a Goliath. And nobody roots for Goliath," he acknowledged.

The NBA — Philadelphia Warriors

In 1959-60, Chamberlain played his first NBA season for the Philadelphia Warriors — the team that had drafted him four years earlier. He did not disappoint his new team, as he averaged 37.6 points and a league-leading 27 rebounds per game. In recognition of the impact he made on the league, Chamberlain was the first player ever to be named NBA rookie of the year, NBA most valuable player, and All-NBA in a single season. In fact, the only weakness anyone could see in the big center's game was his

Chamberlain holding a sign reading "100" in a dressing room in Hershey, PA, after he scored 100 points as the Warriors defeated the New York Knicks 169-147, March 2, 1962

free throw shooting. As a rookie he made only 58 percent of his shots from the charity stripe, which was a real problem since he was fouled so often. "I know the problem is all in my head," Chamberlain admitted. "I shoot free throws well in practice."

Despite Chamberlain's phenomenal talents, however, the Warriors were knocked out of the NBA playoffs that year by the powerful Boston Celtics. It was an early indication of what would happen to the Warriors for the next several years. The Celtics, coached by the legendary Red Auerbach, were a talented and hard-working team that won four NBA championships in five years during the late 1950s and early 1960s. In contrast, the Warriors had an inexperienced coach and a bunch of middle-of-the-road players. But many fans still expected Chamberlain to prevail in his many playoff matchups against Celtics center Bill Russell. In fact, Chamberlain usually posted more points and rebounds than his rival, but the Celtics still won with their better overall talent. "I'd play my heart out against Russell, and someone else on my team would blow the game," he recalled. To make matters worse, the media often characterized Chamberlain as the villain in the rivalry between the two big men. "The world is made up of Davids. I am a Goliath. And nobody roots for Goliath," he acknowledged.

Overall, Chamberlain was unhappy with a number of aspects of his rookie NBA season. "I don't like the way I'm coached," he explained. "I'm not allowed to shoot when I have an open shot. The referees don't call fouls when other players push and shove me. My body aches all over." Then, prior to his second season, the NBA took steps to make it even harder for him to succeed. The league instituted several new rules that were specifically designed to decrease Chamberlain's impact on the game. For example, one rule limited the amount of time a player could stand in the key area around the basket to three seconds, and another rule prohibited players from touching the ball when it was in contact with or directly above their own rim (the resulting violation was known as offensive goal-tending). Chamberlain still managed to claim both the league's scoring and rebounding titles during the 1960-61 season, but the Warriors were eliminated in the first round of the playoffs.

The following year, the team got a new head coach, Frank McGwire. Chamberlain has described McGwire as "the finest man and the best coach I've ever played for." The coach complied with his star player's request to be allowed to play the entire game, and he also made a point of complaining to the referees when Chamberlain took a hard foul. The Warriors also began to realize that Chamberlain could not be expected to carry the team all alone and added two solid guards, Al Attles and Guy Rodgers. As a result of McGwire's support, Chamberlain had one of the best years of his career, averaging an NBA record 50.4 points per game. The highlight of that year—when Chamberlain scored an astounding 100 points in a single game—is still one of basketball's most famous moments.

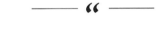

"I like the 100-point game more than I did at the time," he admitted later. *"It has reached fabled proportions, almost like a Paul Bunyan story, and it's nice to be part of a fable."*

The 100-Point Game

By the time Chamberlain notched his 100-point game, many fans had already begun to believe that the 25-year-old Warriors center was capable of such a feat. After all, he had already broken the NBA's single-game scoring record twice that year, with a 73-point performance early in the season and a 78-point game in December. The big event occurred on March 2, 1962, during a game against the New York Knicks that was played in Hershey, Pennsylvania—a small city about an hour from Philadelphia where the Warriors played several games each season. Amazingly enough, the game was attended by only 4,124 fans.

The excitement began to build as Chamberlain scored 23 points in the first quarter and 18 in the second for a total of 41 at the half. By that time, the Warriors led by a score of 79-68. Early in the second half, the Knicks' center got into foul trouble, and then smaller opposing players resorted to fouling Chamberlain almost every time he touched the ball. But Chamberlain was accurate with his free throws for a change, making 13 of 14 in the first half and 15 of 18 in the second. He had 69 points by the beginning of the fourth quarter, and the Warriors led the game by a score of 125-106. When he broke his own single-game scoring record of 78 points with eight minutes left in the game, the small crowd knew that it was witnessing the greatest offensive performance in NBA history.

Of course, the Knicks did not want to be known as the team that allowed a player to score 100 points in a game, so they began holding the ball as long as they could in order to keep it out of Chamberlain's hands. But the big man could not be stopped, and he hit a lay-up with 46 seconds left for his 100th point of the game. The crowd ran onto the court in celebration. No one knows whether Chamberlain could have actually topped 100 points that night, because play was never resumed due to all the commotion.

Afterward, Chamberlain expressed some embarrassment about his performance, since he had taken 63 shots that night. "You take that many shots on the playground and no one ever wants you on their team," he stated. But, years later, he came to appreciate the significance of his achievement. "I like the 100-point game more than I did at the time," he admitted. "It has reached fabled proportions, almost like a Paul Bunyan story, and it's nice to be part of a fable." Still, he gave the game ball from that contest to his former teammate Al Attles—who had made eight of eight shots from the field that night—upon Attles's retirement as head coach of the Golden State Warriors. On the ball, Chamberlain wrote: "To Al, who did everything right at the wrong time." Whenever he was asked what he considered to be the best game of his career, Chamberlain said it was the game on November 24, 1960, when he pulled down 55 rebounds.

Becoming a Team Player

Even though Chamberlain led the league in scoring and rebounding for the third straight year in 1961-62, he still could not lead his team to an NBA title. The Warriors lost to their bitter rivals, the Boston Celtics, in the Eastern Conference finals. In 1962-63 the Warriors moved across the country to San Francisco. After a disappointing season that year, they made it all the way to the NBA finals from the Western Division in 1963-64. Unfortunately, they lost the championship to the Celtics even though Chamberlain outplayed Russell in the final series.

Midway through the 1964-65 season, Chamberlain was traded to the Philadelphia 76ers (formerly the Syracuse Nationals). The 76ers were a solid team with several promising young players, including forwards Luke Jackson and Chet Walker and guards Hal Greer and Larry Costello. They struggled to get used to one another and barely made the playoffs,

Chamberlain celebrating in the 76ers dressing room after Philadelphia defeated the Boston Celtics, 140-116, to win the Eastern Division NBA championship, April 12, 1967

but then they found their stride and made it all the way to the conference finals. Unfortunately, they lost to Chamberlain's old nemesis, the Celtics, in seven games. It was the same story in 1965-66—the 76ers posted the best record in the Eastern Conference during the regular season, and Chamberlain was named the league's most valuable player, but they fell to the Celtics in the playoffs.

The 1966-67 season marked a significant change in Chamberlain's game. The 76ers hired a new coach, Alex Hannum, and added several more gifted young players. Suddenly Chamberlain was no longer the only player on his team who could score. Relieved of this pressure, he demonstrated that he could be an all-around team player by concentrating on rebounding, passing, and defense. That season marked the first time in his career that Chamberlain did not lead the league in scoring. "My scoring went down only because I wanted it to, because it was what was best for my team. I could always score 50-60 points if it was needed, but I knew my team was more effective if I sacrificed my scoring and passed and played defense," he stated.

But Chamberlain happily gave up his personal records in order to achieve team success. The 76ers posted an amazing 68-13 record that year— which was the best in NBA history until the Chicago Bulls broke the record in 1997— defeated the Celtics in the Eastern Conference finals, and beat the San Francisco Warriors to claim the NBA championship. Chamberlain's contributions were recognized when he was named MVP.

The 76ers had another great regular season in 1967-68, and many people expected them to repeat as NBA champions, but they stumbled in the playoffs. Chamberlain demonstrated his versatility that season by leading the league in assists with 702. "I got more happiness out of that record than almost any other record," he recalled. "I showed people I could pass the ball to my teammates. The record proved I was more than a giant who could just dunk the ball. It proved I was willing to share the glory of winning."

Los Angeles Lakers

The following year, Chamberlain was traded to the Los Angeles Lakers. He joined a talented team that included Elgin Baylor and Jerry West. Although Chamberlain had some trouble fitting in at first, the team still made it all the way to the NBA finals, where they lost to the Boston Celtics.

In 1969-70, Chamberlain suffered a knee injury early in the season. It was uncertain whether he would ever be able to play basketball again, but he committed himself to an intensive rehabilitation program and planned to return in time for that season's playoffs. "I had to will myself to get well, all the way well. I really wanted to play basketball again. I wanted to play in less than five months!" he stated. "Whatever they told me to do, I doubled it. If they said I should run five miles, I ran ten. If they said I should lift ten pounds with my leg, I lifted 20." Part of his therapy involved running on the beach, and it was at this time that he first became interested in sand volleyball. "I had the time of my life on the beach in bare feet and a pair of $2.98 shorts. I played volleyball all day, day after day," he recalled. "I found out just how little I really needed to be happy." Chamberlain fulfilled his promise to come back for the playoffs, but the Lakers lost a thrilling seven-game final series to the Knicks. Still, the big center's courage and determination in returning from his injury increased his popularity with fans.

The Lakers had a disappointing 1970-71 season, when many important players went down with injuries. But they came back in 1971-72 to post an impressive 69-13 record during the regular season. At one point, the team won an incredible 33 games in a row. Even though Chamberlain's scoring average dropped to a career low 14.8 points per game, he contributed to the team's success in many other ways. The Lakers made it to the NBA championships, where they took the title from the Knicks in five games. Chamberlain broke his hand in the fourth game of the final series, but he still managed to score 24 points, grab 29 rebounds, and block 10 shots in the deciding fifth game.

Retirement and Legacy

At the end of the 1972-73 season, which saw the Lakers make it to the finals again but lose to the Knicks, Chamberlain announced his retirement from basketball. "I could have signed another contract and made a lot more money," he noted. "In some ways I was getting better as a player. But I no longer found it fun to play. And too many hang on too long." In 14 NBA seasons, Chamberlain set countless records and fundamentally changed the way the game was played. Before his time, professional basketball tended to be rather slow and methodical. But as soon as he entered the league and became the first player to use the dunk as an offensive weapon, the game became fast and exciting.

At the end of the 1972-73 season, which saw the Lakers make it to the finals again but lose to the Knicks, Chamberlain announced his retirement from basketball. "I could have signed another contract and made a lot more money," he noted. "In some ways I was getting better as a player. But I no longer found it fun to play. And too many hang on too long."

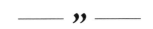

Chamberlain's career average of 30.1 points per game is second only to Michael Jordan's, and he also pulled down nearly 24,000 career rebounds. Chamberlain still holds the NBA records for most points in a single game (100), most rebounds in a game (55), highest scoring average for a season (50.4), most points in a season (4,029), most rebounds in a season (2,149), and most career games without ever fouling out (1,045). "I'm proud of

Chamberlain and Bill Russell laughing as they recall the glory days during a tribute to Russell at the FleetCenter in Boston, May 26, 1999.

that record," he commented about never fouling out of a game. "I get paid to help my team. I can't help them if I'm on the bench or in the shower." In 1978, he was elected to the Basketball Hall of Fame in his first year of eligibility.

The only disappointment in Chamberlain's amazing basketball career was that—despite his dominance on the court—he only won two NBA titles. "Everybody would like to have a few more rings, but I wouldn't trade the experiences I had," he noted. "If you win like that, like the Celtics did, year after year, if you win everything when you're a young man, then you expect to win everything for the rest of your life."

HOME AND FAMILY

Chamberlain never married or had children. "I've never been even close to getting married," he once stated. "I don't have anything against marriage, but I try to be logical in my doings. A lot of people are afraid of being alone, of not being loved. But there isn't any guaranteed security that a family is going to love you. And I've never found anyone I could make a commitment to." Up until his death, he lived on a hilltop in Bel Air, California, in a luxurious, pyramid-shaped home that he helped to design and build in 1971. It featured high ceilings and lots of stained glass, and it was surrounded by a moat.

As a famous bachelor, Chamberlain always had a reputation for dating many attractive women. In 1991, he was criticized for claiming in his autobiography that he had had sexual relations with 20,000 different women. Many people felt that it was irresponsible for Chamberlain to be so promiscuous and that he certainly should not be bragging about it. A short time later, Los Angeles Lakers star Magic Johnson announced that he had tested positive for HIV—the virus that causes AIDS. Chamberlain then became involved in a controversy involving athletes and other supposed role models not practicing safe sex. "I tell people—and I'm remiss for not doing so in the book—that I definitely believe there's a need for safe sex," he responded. "I was fortunate enough to be in my prime in the '60s and '70s, when there was a sexual revolution for women and there wasn't the concern about AIDS and these social diseases that are so very scary."

HOBBIES AND OTHER INTERESTS

After his retirement from basketball, Chamberlain remained involved in a wide variety of sports as a participant, coach, and sponsor. His favorite sports to play included volleyball, waterskiing, tennis, polo, swimming, running, and rowing. He also sponsored and coached volleyball and track teams, providing support for young athletes who were training to compete in the Olympics. He was also active in Special Olympics and other charities that help children. Outside of sports, Chamberlain enjoyed traveling, listening to jazz music, and collecting cars. "I've never had any bad habits for spending money except on cars," he noted. Shortly before he died, he was learning to play the saxophone and trying to become comfortable with his computer.

In the early 1990s, Chamberlain decided to try making a career for himself as an actor. His first part was in *Conan the Destroyer,* an action movie in which he got to fight Arnold Schwarzenegger. "I've always been interested in movies," Chamberlain stated. "*Conan* is not the sort of film I'd go to, but I wanted to have a chance to see how the whole thing is done."

"I've lost a dear and exceptional friend and an important part of my life," said his longtime rival Bill Russell. *"We just loved playing against each other. The fierceness of the competition bonded us as friends for eternity."*

DEATH

Chamberlain remained very active in amateur sports and in charity work in the years following his retirement. So it came as a shock to his many friends and fans when he died on October 12, 1999, at the age of 63. According to his friend and attorney Seymour Goldberg, Chamberlain suffered from congestive heart failure and deteriorated quickly during the last few months of his life, losing 40 to 50 pounds and complaining of extreme pain.

In the days following his death, numerous people stepped forward to tell what he had meant to them and to the game of basketball. "I've lost a dear and exceptional friend and an important part of my life," said his longtime rival Bill Russell. "We just loved playing against each other. The fierceness of the competition bonded us as friends for eternity." "Wilt was one of the greatest ever, and we will never see another one like him," added Kareem Abdul-Jabbar, who broke Chamberlain's career scoring record. "We've lost a giant of a man in every sense of the word," said NBA Commissioner David Stern. "The shadow of accomplishment he cast over our game is unlikely ever to be matched."

WRITINGS

Wilt: Just Like Any Other Seven-Foot Black Millionaire Who Lives Next Door, 1973 (with David Shaw)
A View from Above, 1991

HONORS AND AWARDS

NCAA All-American: 1956-57, 1957-58
NCAA Tournament Most Valuable Player: 1956-57
NBA Rookie of the Year: 1959-60
NBA Most Valuable Player: 1959-60, 1965-66, 1966-67, 1967-68
NBA Points Leader: 1959-66
NBA Rebound Leader: 1959-63, 1965-69, 1970-73
NBA Assist Leader: 1967-68
NBA Hall of Fame: 1978

FURTHER READING

Books

Chamberlain, Wilt. *A View from Above,* 1991

Chamberlain, Wilt, with David Shaw. *Wilt: Just Like Any Other Seven-Foot Black Millionaire Who Lives Next Door,* 1973

Contemporary Authors, Vol. 103

Frankl, Ron. *Basketball Legends: Wilt Chamberlain,* 1995 (juvenile)

Hahn, James, and Lynn Hahn. *Wilt! The Sports Career of Wilton Chamberlain,* 1981 (juvenile)

Nadel, Eric. *The Night Wilt Scored 100,* 1990

Rudeen, Kenneth. *Wilt Chamberlain,* 1970 (juvenile)

Who's Who in America, 1999

World Book Encyclopedia 1999

Periodicals

Boston Globe, Oct. 13, 1999, p.A1

Current Biography Yearbook 1960

Detroit Free Press, Oct. 13, 1999, p.A1

Esquire, May 1988, p.53

Jet, Mar. 16, 1992, p.48; Jan. 30, 1995, p.50

Los Angeles Times, Oct. 13, 1999, p.A1; Oct. 14, 1999, p.D1

Maclean's, Nov. 18, 1991, p.84

New York Times, Oct. 13, 1999, pp.A1, D3

People, July 30, 1984, p.43

Philadelphia Inquirer, Oct. 13, 1999, p.A1; Oct. 17, 1999, p.A1

Sport, Dec. 1986, p.49

Sporting News, May 28, 1984, p.10

Sports Illustrated, Aug. 18, 1986, p.62; Mar. 2, 1987, p.6; Apr. 1, 1991, p.84; Dec. 9, 1991, p.22; Oct. 25, 1999, p.80

Time, Oct. 25, 1999, p.142

WORLD WIDE WEB SITE

http://www.nba.com/history/chamberlain_bio.html

http://www.nbaat50/greats/chamberlain.html

Brandi Chastain 1968-

American Professional Soccer Player
Olympic Gold Medalist in 1996
Member of the Women's World Cup Championship
Team in 1999

BIRTH

Brandi Denise Chastain was born on July 21, 1968, in San
Jose, California. She was the oldest of two children born to
Roger and Lark Chastain. She has a younger brother, Chad.

YOUTH

Growing up in San Jose, Chastain was a very active girl. She played house with her girlfriends, but she mostly enjoyed playing sports with her brother and the neighborhood boys. She spent a great deal of time climbing trees, jumping fences, and trying to hit a baseball over the roof of the house across the street. "I played just about everything when I was younger—football, baseball—everything," she recalled. "I don't know why, but the first time I got hold of a soccer ball, I was hooked."

Chastain began playing soccer at the age of six. When she was eight, she joined her first soccer team. The team was called the Quakettes, after a local professional soccer team called the San Jose Earthquakes. One time, Chastain and her team appeared in a halftime exhibition game during an Earthquakes match. "When I was a kid growing up in San Jose, my favorite thing to do was to go to Earthquakes games," she noted. "My greatest memory was playing at halftime and hearing the crowd cheer when I scored a goal."

> *"I played just about everything when I was younger—football, baseball—everything. I don't know why, but the first time I got hold of a soccer ball, I was hooked."*

When Chastain was around 10, she joined a traveling soccer team called the Horizons. Her father coached the team, while her mother acted as the head cheerleader along the sidelines. Sometimes, Lark Chastain would embarrass her daughter by yelling encouragement through a megaphone. But Brandi appreciated the support she received from her family. For example, her grandfather rewarded her for hard work and unselfish play on the soccer field. "He'd pay me a dollar for goals, but when I made an assist, he paid me a dollar fifty!" she remembered.

By the time Chastain turned 12, her impressive soccer skills had attracted the attention of the Olympic Development Program. This program sponsors a network of state and regional teams that develop promising young players for the U.S. National Team, which represents the country in the Olympics and other international competitions. Over the next few years, Chastain moved up the ranks of the program. At the age of 16, she was invited to attend the national team camp.

EDUCATION

Chastain was a good student at Archbishop Mitty High School in San Jose. Her favorite subjects were science and math, and she also enjoyed reading Shakespeare. "I know a lot of kids think 'Shakespeare? Yuck!' But I've always loved it," she stated. Chastain also starred on her high school soccer team. In fact, she led her team to three consecutive state championships before she graduated in 1986.

That fall, Chastain enrolled in the University of California at Berkeley. During her freshman year, she played soccer on the Berkeley team, which also included her future Olympic and World Cup teammate Joy Fawcett. But Chastain admits that she was not prepared for the freedom of college. She concentrated too much on soccer and not enough on her classes. "I went from a small Catholic high school to this huge university," she explained. "Some of my classes had 800 students in them. I figured the professor would never know if I was there, so I'd skip class figuring I'd catch up tomorrow. It didn't happen that way."

By the end of her freshman year, Chastain's grades had slipped so much that she ended up on academic probation. To make matters worse, she tore ligaments in her knee during spring soccer practice. The injury required surgery and kept her out of action for the season. At this point, she decided to drop out of Berkeley and attend a junior college, Merritt College, closer to home. After one year at Merritt, she transferred to Santa Clara University. Santa Clara turned out to be a better fit for Chastain. She led the women's soccer team to the semifinals of the NCAA tournament in each of her two years there, 1989 and 1990. She also met her future husband, Jerry Smith, who coached men's soccer at the university. Chastain earned her bachelor's degree in communications in 1990.

CAREER HIGHLIGHTS

1991 Women's World Cup

Chastain first joined the U.S. Women's National Soccer Team in 1988, during her year at Merritt College. Unfortunately, she suffered another knee injury during her first appearance in an international match. But she rejoined the national team in 1991, after she had finished her college soccer career. She was thrilled to have the opportunity to play in the first-ever Women's World Cup tournament that year.

The World Cup has been one of the premier events in men's soccer since the early 20th century. Countries around the world form national teams composed of their best players. These teams compete in a series of qualifying matches, and the top 24 teams advance to the World Cup tournament, which takes place every four years. The men's World Cup is the most popular sporting event in the world. But women's soccer is a fairly recent addition to these international competitions. The first Women's World Cup was held in China in 1991.

Chastain played some of her earliest games with the U.S. Women's National Soccer Team during the qualifying rounds of this tournament. Since she did not have much experience with the team, her playing time was limited. As a result, she became very nervous each time she went onto the field. Her nervous energy led to one of the most embarrassing moments of her soccer career. During one game, the coaches put her in at halftime. Shortly after taking the field, she received a pass and realized that she was wide open, with no opposing players between her and the goal.

"I got a through ball and nobody was in front of me. I was about 45 yards from the goal and I took a really long dribble," she recalled. "As I got closer to the goal, I thought, 'I'm going to kick the ball so hard I'm going to knock the goalkeeper into the back of the net.' I wound up, took a swing—I'm sure the back of my heel must have touched my ear, that's how much of a backswing I had—and completely missed the ball! I took out a divot bigger than any golfer has ever taken! It was probably a good yard long." After the game, one of her teammates jokingly presented her with the strip of grass she had dislodged as a keepsake.

> *Chastain's nervous energy led to one of the most embarrassing moments of her soccer career. "I got a through ball and nobody was in front of me. . . . As I got closer to the goal, I thought, 'I'm going to kick the ball so hard I'm going to knock the goalkeeper into the back of the net.' I wound up, took a swing—I'm sure the back of my heel must have touched my ear, that's how much of a backswing I had—and completely missed the ball! I took out a divot bigger than any golfer has ever taken! It was probably a good yard long."*

But Chastain soon recovered from that experience and began showing the world her abilities. In a World Cup qualifying match against Mexico, for example, she set a new American record by scoring five consecutive goals. The U.S. women's team went on to win the World Cup. Unfortunately, Chastain suffered another knee injury a short time later and had to take time off for surgery.

Dropped from the U.S. National Team

In 1993, Chastain received disappointing news from Anson Dorrance, the head coach of the U.S. Women's National Soccer Team. Dorrance told Chastain that, because of her frequent injuries and the number of other talented players available at her position, she no longer had a spot on the team. But Chastain was determined to continue playing and improving in hopes of one day returning to the national team.

"Brandi can do so many things well," said coach Tony DiCicco. "She heads the ball as well as anyone else on the team; she's a good tackler; she holds the ball well and can pass under pressure well. [She's] a world-class defender and one of the best players in the world."

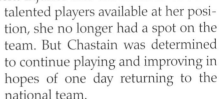

After being dropped from the U.S. team, Chastain played professional soccer in Japan for two seasons. She was named the most valuable player on her team, called the Shiroki Serena, and became the only foreign player named among the top ten players in the league. Chastain also became an assistant soccer coach with Santa Clara University and played with a top club team, the Sacramento Storm.

For Chastain, the most difficult part of her time away from the national team came in 1995, during the second Women's World Cup. She was forced to watch on television while her friends on the U.S. team finished a disappointing third in the tournament, behind Norway and Sweden. "It was tough because as a player, you want to be there," she noted.

Changes Positions from Forward to Defender

The following year, the national team began training for the 1996 Olympic Games. This competition, held in Atlanta, Georgia, would mark the first time that women's soccer had been included as a medal sport in the Olympics. The U.S. team's new coach, Tony DiCicco, contacted Chastain and invited her to try out for the team again. But there was a catch. He wanted her to move from forward—the position she had always played—to defender. Still, Chastain jumped at the chance. "Tony said that I was good enough to be on the team, but we had too many forwards," she recalled. "He said he'd find a position for me, but it might be in the back. So I said, 'Well, if it keeps me on the field, that's all that matters.'"

As a forward, Chastain's main responsibility had been trying to score goals. She was able to take chances with the ball because she was usually in the other team's end of the field. But as a defender, she had to learn to be more patient, control the play, and protect her own goal. "Defenders are a team's safety valves," she explained. "When you play defense, your job is to settle things down, redistribute, or get the team out of tough situations. Midfield defenders create the calm before the 'flashes' up front storm through and score."

As the U.S. team continued to train for the Olympics, it became clear that the coach had made a good decision by switching Chastain to defense. She adapted well to the new position and even came to enjoy it. "I almost feel better playing in that position because I get to see the whole field. I get to run forward with the ball. I get to pick and choose when I get to attack," she stated. "The forwards get a lot of glory because they score and they do some great things, but it's my responsibility to make sure the ball gets up there, to give support to those players, maybe make runs off the ball to open up some space. So it's really a creative position."

By the time the U.S. team went to Atlanta for the Olympics, Chastain was recognized as a smart and versatile player and a leader on the field. "Brandi can do so many things well," said DiCicco. "She heads the ball as well as anyone else on the team; she's a good tackler; she holds the ball well and can pass under pressure well. [She's] a world-class defender and one of the best players in the world."

The 1996 Olympic Games

The U.S. women's team was one of the favorites to win the gold medal in the 1996 Olympics. During the first match against Denmark, Chastain got an assist on the first goal ever scored in women's Olympic soccer history. She threw the ball inbounds to her teammate Tisha Venturini, who scored a goal. The Americans went on to beat Denmark 3-0 in that game. They followed that win with a 2-1 victory over Sweden and a 0-0 tie with China in the opening round.

The U.S. women faced Norway in the semifinals for the right to play in the gold medal match. In the middle of an intense game, Chastain injured her knee again. "When the doctor checked Brandi's knee on the sideline, he said she could still play, if she could tolerate the pain," her husband recalled. "She was OK moving in a straight line or while using her left leg, but she couldn't pass with the inside of her right foot, and she was unable to make the overlapping runs from the back that she had previously." But Chastain still wanted to play, and the coaches decided that she could still help the team despite her injury. The U.S. team ended up defeating Norway 2-1 in overtime to make it to the finals.

In the gold medal match, the American women faced China for a second time. The teams seemed very evenly matched: both had emerged from the preliminary rounds with 2-0-1 records, including a 0-0 tie against each other. The game was an intense, defensive matchup. When it was all over, the Americans claimed the first-ever Olympic gold medal in women's soccer by a score of 2-1. Despite her injury, Chastain played every minute of the Olympics. With her help, the U.S. defense allowed only three goals in the entire tournament. At the gold medal ceremony, Chastain proudly threw her head back and sang the national anthem at the top of her lungs.

Chastain and the other players were particularly pleased because they won the gold medal in front of the largest crowd ever to watch a women's sporting event anywhere in the world. Before the Olympics, the largest crowd to attend one of the U.S. National Team's matches had been only 7,000. Yet few television viewers had seen the event.

After that game, many people expressed frustration because NBC, the TV network broadcasting the Olympics, had shown only a few minutes of the championship game. The network obviously didn't think many viewers cared about women's soccer. Yet 76,481 fans turned out to watch the U.S. victory over China. It was a milestone for women's sports, the largest crowd ever — anywhere in the world — to see a women's soccer event, and the largest crowd in the U.S. to see any women's sporting event.

The 1999 Women's World Cup

Shortly after their gold medal triumph, the U.S. National Team began training for the 1999 Women's World Cup soccer tournament. They hoped to improve upon their disappointing third place finish in 1995, when Chastain had not been part of the team. They also hoped that the World Cup would continue to attract new American fans to women's soccer, since it was scheduled to be held in the United States.

Chastain and the other players on the women's national soccer team became such awesome athletes through hard work and training. Between big events like the World Cup or the Olympics, they play together as a team in competitions against the top international teams in stadiums around the world. But they also have a training camp in Orlando, Florida, where the team spends five or six months working together to get ready for the big events. It's tough for the players to be away from their homes and families for extended periods like that. Many are married, and two — Carla Overbeck and Joy Fawcett — are mothers of young children. Their kids spend a lot of time at the training camp with them, with a nanny on duty to help out.

"I almost feel better playing defender because I get to see the whole field. I get to run forward with the ball. I get to pick and choose when I get to attack. The forwards get a lot of glory because they score and they do some great things, but it's my responsibility to make sure the ball gets up there, to give support to those players, maybe make runs off the ball to open up some space. So it's really a creative position."

In Florida, their training complex has four soccer fields, offices, and apartments and houses nearby. The team members live together in small groups, sharing companionship and fun. They start their workouts early in the morning, to avoid some of the intense midday Florida heat and humidity. Their workouts include drills in speed, endurance, strength, conditioning, and specific soccer skills. In addition to practice, they have team meetings and do a lot of weight lifting. Still, there's a lot of down time, for hanging out with roommates and analyzing what worked and what didn't in practice. Equally important, they're building team cohesiveness, taking individual players and forming them into one tight team. They have a sports psychologist who helps them work on team-building exercises—things like forming two teams, holding hands, and then trying to get the whole team through a hula hoop without letting go of each other. The exercises seem goofy, but they offer lessons in communication, leadership, unity, and trust

As the 1999 Women's World Cup approached, Chastain became one of the best-known players on the team. Always an enthusiastic promoter of soccer, she did a number of different things to attract publicity to the tournament. For example, Chastain raised some eyebrows by appearing nude—but carefully hidden behind a soccer ball—in a print advertisement. Afterwards, she was invited to be a guest on David Letterman's late-night TV talk show. Chastain charmed Letterman, who told her that he thought the U.S. women's soccer team was "Babe City." "I love being a little crazy—some would say strange—off the field," Chastain admitted, "but it's all business between the lines."

> *"After I put my head down, I looked up, and standing over me was my captain, Carla Overbeck. She looked at me and said, 'Brandi, this game has 85 minutes left. Let's go. You are going to be the difference in this game.' And with that trust, I made it through the first half and ended up scoring a goal to tie the game, and we went on to win, 3-2. I don't think without that encouragement I would have made it through the game."*

The Women's World Cup tournament featured 16 teams from around the world. These teams played a total of 32 matches over a three week period in stadiums around the United States. Each team played three games in the opening round, then the top teams advanced through the quarterfinals, semifinals, and finals. The American team won their first game of the opening round against Denmark, 3-0, in front of a record crowd of 79,000 fans. They went on to beat Nigeria, 7-1, and South Korea, 3-0, to remain undefeated in opening round action.

During the quarterfinals against Germany, Chastain had one of her worst moments of the tournament. She scored an own-goal, meaning that she accidentally knocked the ball into the U.S. net and scored for the other team. Her mistake gave Germany a 1-0 lead. She put her head down in disgust, but her teammates wouldn't let her dwell on it. "After I put my head down, I looked up, and standing over me was my captain, Carla Overbeck," Chastain remembered. "She looked at me and said, 'Brandi, this game has 85 minutes left. Let's go. You are going to be the difference in this game.' And with that trust, I made it through the first half and ended up scoring a goal to tie the game, and we went on to win, 3-2. I don't think without that encouragement I would have made it through the game."

The U.S. team went on to the finals, playing China for the World Cup championship at the Rose Bowl stadium in Pasadena, California, in front of 90,185 fans, another new record for women's sports. The two teams were evenly matched, and they both played an aggressive but controlled game. Both defensive lines were so strong that despite numerous opportunities, neither team was able to score during regulation play (90 minutes). The game went into two 15-minute overtime periods, and play was intense as both teams tried for the winning goal. Still, neither

Chastain, center, celebrates with teammates Sara Whalen, left, and Shannon MacMillan after kicking the game-winning overtime penalty shootout goal against China during the Women's World Cup final, July 10, 1999.

team was able to score during either the first or the second overtime, and the game went into a penalty kick shoot-out. For each team, five players would come up one at a time to the line, 12 feet out, and have a chance to shoot on goal. For the U.S., the shooters would be Carla Overbeck, Joy Fawcett, Kristine Lilly, Mia Hamm, and Brandi Chastain. The pressure was enormous, both on the shooters and on U.S. goalie Briana Scurry and the Chinese goalkeeper, Gao Hong. And the odds favor the shooters.

The two teams alternated shots, with China going first. The first four kickers—two for each team—all found the goal. But then China's third shooter, midfielder Liu Ying, came up to the line. "I saw her body language when she was walking up to the penalty spot," Scurry said. "She didn't look like she really wanted to be there. Her shoulders were slumped, and she looked tired. I thought, 'This is the one.'" She was sure that this was the one goal she would be able to block. As Liu approached the ball, Scurry sprang forward and to her left, blocking the shot. So when the U. S. made their third goal, they were now up one. Both China and the U.S. made their fourth shots, and then China made a goal on its fifth shot. Now it was up to the final U.S. shooter, Brandi Chastain.

Chastain usually took penalty shots with her dominant right foot. But during practice, the U.S. coaches had noticed that her right-footed penalty shots usually went in the same direction. They felt this might give the opposing goaltender a better chance to block the ball. To compensate, Chastain practiced making penalty kicks with her left foot. This practice paid off. Chastain barely hesitated before she used her left foot to fire the last American shot past Chinese goaltender Gao Hong for a 5-4 overtime win. "I didn't hear any noise. I didn't look at the [Chinese goaltender]," she recalled. "As soon as the whistle blew, I just stepped up and hit it."

Although Chastain has enjoyed all the attention, she emphasizes that she does not want to be known only for removing her shirt. "It was in Technicolor. It was in your face. It was highlighted, and that's OK. But I don't want it to overshadow everything else."

After scoring the goal that gave her team the World Cup championship, Chastain dropped to her knees, whipped off her shirt, and twirled it above her head in celebration. The photograph of this moment—with Chastain in her black Nike sports bra—appeared in newspapers and on magazine covers all around the country. Afterward, a few people criticized Chastain for taking off her shirt. Some claimed that her behavior was inappropriate, while others speculated that it was planned as a free advertisement for Nike. But Chastain insisted that it was a genuine, spontaneous expression of her emotions at the time. "Momentary insanity, nothing more, nothing less," she stated. "I thought, My God, this is the greatest moment of my life on a soccer field! I just lost my head." For many fans, the picture of the triumphant Chastain is an exuberant portrait of the power and beauty of women's athletics.

Connecting with Fans

More than 41 million people watched the U.S. women's triumph in the 1999 World Cup on television. Chastain and her teammates were thrilled

Chastain celebrates after kicking the winning penalty shot to win the 1999 Women's World Cup final against China, July 10, 1999.

with the increased attention their victory brought to the game of soccer. Thanks to her game-winning goal and the famous photograph, Chastain emerged as one of the highest-profile members of the team.

Although Chastain has enjoyed all the attention, she emphasizes that she does not want to be known only for removing her shirt. "It was in Technicolor. It was in your face. It was highlighted, and that's ok," she noted.

35

Chastain signs autographs for a group of young fans.

"But I don't want it to overshadow everything else." Instead, she hopes to build on the success of the 1999 Women's World Cup to attract new players and fans to soccer in the United States. She wants to share her love of the game, and also to encourage American girls to play soccer so that there will be a new generation of stars to represent the country in future competitions. "I have a responsibility to make kids feel the same way about [soccer] as I did as a kid," she stated. "We have to teach young players the dedication that's needed to be on the team. . . . Our team depends on those people who have those characteristics."

Since the World Cup, Chastain has become a spokesperson for her teammates and for women's soccer. It is a role that she thoroughly enjoys. "I'm a proponent of women's soccer. Any time there's a question posed and everyone looks around the room, I'll be the first to stand up and say how I feel about the game, how I feel about my teammates. I want people to listen, and I want us to be heard," she noted. "I love preaching the word of soccer. It's not because I have to do it; it's because I choose to."

Chastain hopes to remain with the U.S. Women's National Soccer Team and play in the 2000 Olympic Games in Sydney, Australia. She anticipates that the team will have a tough fight to defend its gold medal. "[It will be] our biggest challenge yet," she admitted. "Everyone wants to kick our butt and is putting more money into the sport." Chastain also plans to participate in a new professional women's soccer league in the United States. Known as the Women's United Soccer Alliance or WUSA, the league will include eight to 10 teams. Play is scheduled to begin in 2001.

MARRIAGE AND FAMILY

Brandi Chastain married Jerry Smith, who is a soccer coach at Santa Clara University, on June 8, 1996. Their wedding was held at the university's historic mission chapel. But Chastain's busy schedule left no time for a honeymoon. The day after the wedding, she returned to on-site training for the 1996 Olympics. They finally went to Paris for a honeymoon two years later, but they spent half of their time there watching men's World Cup soccer matches.

"I'm a proponent of women's soccer. Any time there's a question posed and everyone looks around the room, I'll be the first to stand up and say how I feel about the game, how I feel about my teammates. I want people to listen, and I want us to be heard. I love preaching the word of soccer. It's not because I have to do it; it's because I choose to."

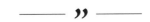

HOBBIES AND OTHER INTERESTS

When she is not training or playing soccer, Chastain loves shopping, especially for shoes. She also enjoys reading, watching movies, and playing golf. "I like working with my hands and teaching myself new things," she noted. "I love traveling. I read all the time."

HONORS AND AWARDS

NCAA First Team All-American: 1990
ISAA National Player of the Year: 1990
World Cup Soccer: 1991, Gold Medal; 1999, Gold Medal
Olympic Soccer: 1996, Gold Medal
Goodwill Games:: 1998, Gold Medal
All-World Cup Team (*Sports Illustrated*): 1999

FURTHER READING

Books

Miller, Marla. *All-American Girls: The U.S. Women's National Soccer Team,* 1999 (juvenile)
Who's Who in America, 2000
Woolum, Janet. *Outstanding Women Athletes,* 1998

Periodicals

Chicago Tribune, Aug. 1, 1996, p.N1; June 27, 1999, p.5, sec. Sports
Daily News of Los Angeles, July 4, 1999, p.S3
Los Angeles Times, July 22, 1996, p.S4; Aug. 2, 1996, p.S1
New York Times, July 22, 1996, p.C3; July 5, 1999, p.D1; July 11, 1999, p.A1
Newsday, Feb. 3, 2000, p.A74
Newsweek, July 19, 1999, p.46
People, Dec. 31, 1999, p.101
Philadelphia Inquirer, Nov. 13, 1999, p.D1
Richmond Times Dispatch, Mar. 2, 2000, p.C1
St. Louis Post-Dispatch, June 18, 1999, p.F1
San Francisco Chronicle, May 8, 1997, p.D1; June 15, 1999, p.B6; July 3, 1999, p.E1
Soccer Jr., Nov. 1998, p.22
Sports Illustrated, Aug. 12, 1996, p.70; July 12, 1999, p.37; July 19, 1999, p.38
Time, July 19, 1999, p.58
USA Today, Nov. 15, 1991, p.C9; Jan. 9, 1996, p.C11; Feb. 16, 2000, p.C14

ADDRESS

U.S. Soccer
1801 S. Prairie Ave.
Chicago, IL 60616

WORLD WIDE WEB SITES

http://www.soccer.com
http://www.womensoccer.com/biogs/chastain

Derek Jeter 1974-

American Professional Baseball Player with the New
York Yankees
1996 American League Rookie of the Year
1999 Gold Glove Award Winner

BIRTH

Derek Sanderson Jeter (GEE-ter) was born on June 26, 1974,
in Pequannock, New Jersey. His father, Charles, was a sub-
stance-abuse counselor, and his mother, Dorothy, was an ac-
countant. Derek has a younger sister named Sharlee.

YOUTH

When Jeter was five, his family moved from New Jersey to Kalamazoo, Michigan. Most kids in Michigan root for the Detroit Tigers baseball team, but Derek was always a New York Yankees fan. Each summer, when he spent time in New Jersey with grandparents or aunts and uncles, he went to lots of Yankees games. "I was always a big David Winfield fan," he recalled, talking about the former star outfielder for the Yankees. In fact, Jeter had a poster of Winfield on his bedroom wall.

During elementary school, Jeter was already telling everyone that he wanted to be a Yankees shortstop when he grew up. His father had been a shortstop for Fisk University in Nashville, Tennessee. "That's why I always wanted to be a shortstop," he explains. "You know, when you're a kid, you want to be just like your dad."

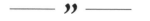

"My parents always felt that if I worked hard enough I could make any dream come true. My upbringing was like **The Cosby Show.** *My parents were involved in everything my sister and I did. I won't brag about me, but I'll brag about my family forever."*

The Jeters' house happened to be right next to a high school baseball field. Often the whole family would jump the fence and take turns hitting and fielding grounders. Because Jeter's father had been a shortstop himself, he was able to coach Derek and help him learn the fundamentals of the position. "It was a position I knew and played, so it was a position I could teach him," Charles Jeter recalled. Derek also got lots of hitting practice. "I would go out and hit a lot of grounders," he remembered. "My mom and sister would be in the outfield and would flag down all the balls I would hit."

Both parents gave Derek lots of encouragement in baseball, school, and life. "My parents always felt that if I worked hard enough I could make any dream come true," he recalled. "My upbringing was like *The Cosby Show*. My parents were involved in everything my sister and I did. I won't brag about me, but I'll brag about my family forever."

At the same time, though, Jeter's parents also made sure he worked to make his dreams come true. Every year, his parents drew up a contract with their two children that would set goals for the coming school year.

For Jeter, being able to play baseball was a reward for meeting a goal such as doing well in school, getting his chores and studying done, or treating friends well. "He knew if he wanted to play in the Little League all-star game, or go to baseball camp," his mother explained, "he better come home with a 4.0 [grade point average], he better have his behavior intact, he better make curfew or he wasn't going anywhere."

Jeter's father was his coach for a while in Little League. To his disappointment, Jeter found himself assigned to second base instead of shortstop. This was his father's way of showing Derek that nothing should be taken for granted. If he wanted to be shortstop, he would have to prove that he could perform well enough to earn the job.

For a long time Derek's father won any kind of game they played together, such as basketball or even checkers. "That's why I'm so competitive," Jeter explained. "He never let up on me." Then one day, when he was in eighth grade, Derek challenged his father to a game of one-on-one basketball. He had learned some new moves and felt he could finally beat his dad. The two made an occasion of it by going to a court at nearby Western Michigan University in Kalamazoo, with Derek's mother coming along to watch. It was a tough game, but Derek won. Afterward, Charles Jeter spoke of the day with pride. "Derek always had the desire to be the best," he remembered.

> *For Jeter, being able to play baseball was a reward for meeting a goal such as doing well in school, getting his chores and studying done, or treating friends well. "He knew if he wanted to play in the Little League all-star game, or go to baseball camp," his mother explained, "he better come home with a 4.0 [grade point average], he better have his behavior intact, he better make curfew or he wasn't going anywhere."*

Because Jeter's father is black and his mother is white, some people think that he must have endured taunts from other kids with prejudiced attitudes. But Jeter says that "it wasn't a problem for me at all. I can relate to everyone—I had friends of all races—black, white, Spanish, whatever." Jeter is proud and appreciative of the way he was raised.

EDUCATION

Jeter attended the public schools in Kalamazoo and went to Kalamazoo Central High School. His high school teachers remember him as a good student—he kept a near-A average—who didn't fit the usual "jock" label. For example, he was known for writing thoughtful essays and reports and for expressing himself well in class.

Jeter played both baseball and basketball in high school. He earned a starting position as shooting guard on the varsity basketball team. On the baseball field, he quickly impressed Coach Norm Copeland at the junior varsity tryouts. "From the first time I saw him throw, I knew I wouldn't be able to keep him on junior varsity for long," Copeland remembered.

> *Although he was the school baseball star, Jeter didn't act cocky. "As we talked as a team or in the locker room before and after games, Derek never centered conversation around himself. He was always focused on the team," said Don Zomer, his varsity coach. "I don't like people who go around talking about themselves," Jeter noted. "My parents made sure I didn't get a big head."*

Before the end of his freshman year, Jeter was on the varsity team. Even the team's senior shortstop, an all-conference star, recognized Jeter's talent and volunteered to move to third base so Jeter could take over his position. Jeter hit .557 in his junior year, so the opposing pitchers began giving him very few pitches he could hit. Yet he still posted a .508 batting average as a senior, striking out only once. He also had 23 runs batted in (RBIs) in 21 games, and stole 12 bases in 12 attempts despite an ankle injury.

Although he was the school baseball star, Jeter didn't act cocky. "As we talked as a team or in the locker room before and after games, Derek never centered conversation around himself. He was always focused on the *team*," said Don Zomer, his varsity coach. "I don't like people who go around talking about themselves," Jeter noted. "My parents made sure I didn't get a big head."

Jeter's performance in high school baseball attracted the attention of scouts for all the major league teams. Sometimes there were as many as 40 scouts attending his games. Scouts assign scores to a player to indicate

Jeter jumps over Seattle Mariners Rich Amaral (8) after forcing him out at second base and throwing to first base to complete a double play, August 16, 1996.

his potential. Anyone with a score of 50 or higher is sure to get a close look by major league ball clubs. During his senior year, Jeter's score was 55. He received glowing reviews in several scouting magazines, as well as a number of awards. For example, *Scholastic Coach Magazine* gave him the Gatorade Award as Michigan's top high school baseball player, and the Michigan High School Coaches' Association voted him player of the year. When the time of his graduation approached in 1992, Jeter initially planned to attend college—he had Florida State, Western Michigan University, and the University of Michigan in mind. However, he set these plans aside as it became increasingly certain that he would be picked early in the major league draft.

CAREER HIGHLIGHTS

The Draft

As draft day approached, some scouts leaked the news that Jeter would probably be picked fifth. The fifth selection was held by the Cincinnati Reds, a team that already had a fine shortstop in Barry Larkin. Although Jeter admired Larkin, he did not like the idea of spending several years as a backup. Then a reporter covering the Houston Astros, the team that had the first pick, wrote a story claiming that the Astros would likely take Jeter. Though he would have felt special to be the first pick in the draft, what Jeter really wanted was to be picked by the Yankees, who had the sixth choice.

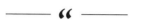

When the phone rang at the Jeter house, it was the New York Yankees. They had selected Jeter with the sixth pick in the draft. "Oh man, I can't even describe how I felt," Jeter remembered. "It was a dream come true, because this is what I always wanted to do."

Draft day that year was June 1, 1992, and the Jeter family waited anxiously for someone to call with the news. The Houston Astros selected Phil Nevin, an outfielder from California. Then the Cleveland Indians, Montreal Expos, Baltimore Orioles, and Cincinnati Reds made their choices. When the phone rang at the Jeter house, it was the New York Yankees. They had selected Jeter with the sixth pick in the draft. "Oh man, I can't even describe how I felt," Jeter remembered. "It was a dream come true, because this is what I always wanted to do."

Jeter's parents were thrilled that he was going to play pro ball. But even though they had great confidence in their son, they knew that a baseball career could not be taken for granted. After all, Derek could get injured, or he might decide he didn't like pro baseball, or the Yankees might lose interest in him. If any of these things happened, he would still need a college education. So Charles and Dorothy Jeter insisted on one condition: the Yankees must pay for his college education, no matter when he started college or how long it took for him to earn a degree. The Yankees agreed, and Jeter went off to play for their minor league team in Tampa, Florida.

The Minor Leagues

It was not easy for the 18-year-old Jeter to leave his family, school, and friends and live on his own in a faraway place. In fact, he was so homesick that he called his parents nearly every night. The stress of leaving home and making major changes to his lifestyle took a toll on the field. On his first playing day, he went hitless in seven times at a bat in a doubleheader. His batting average at the end of the 1992 season was only .202.

The next season, his hitting improved to .295, but his fielding began to decline. "I was making errors every day," he recalled. "I was saying, 'Maybe they won't hit another ball to shortstop,' and it was only the first two weeks of the season." Jeter made 56 errors in his second season, and his coaches began talking about converting him to an outfielder.

Part of the problem was that Jeter was underweight. "I wouldn't have drafted me," he said later. "I weighed 156 pounds fully dressed. . . . I figured when I got on the scale at Tampa they would just send me home." His conditioning coach, Shawn Powell, recalled that "clothes just hung off him. I called him Gilligan in the Skipper's clothes." To address the problem, Powell put Jeter on an off-season diet and exercise program that added 40 pounds of muscle without reducing his quickness.

Climbing Up the Minors

The training program added to Jeter's growing confidence, and he heeded his parents' advice to "stick with it." In 1994, his third season in the minors, he did so well that by June he was promoted from the Class A team in Tampa to the Class AA team in Albany, New York. Jeter didn't stay long in Albany—just long enough to be named Eastern League Player of the Month in July. He batted .377 in 34 games, then got promoted again. This time it was to the Columbus Clippers, the Class AAA team just below the Yankees. He finished 1994 with a .344 average, playing through three levels of minor league in a single season. As Clippers manager Stump Merrill recalled, "The kid [came] in and looked like he belonged from the day he got here."

In a normal season, Jeter would have joined the Yankees at the beginning of September, when they were able to expand the roster for the playoffs.

Jeter hitting a two-run homer against the Seattle Mariners, August 29, 1998.

But the 1994 baseball season was shortened by a players' strike. The end of the season was canceled, along with the playoffs and World Series. Jeter was asked if he would be willing to be a "replacement player" if the strike was not resolved in time for the 1995 season. "Never," he responded. "The players are striking for the future of the game. I don't see the sense in going against them." He knew that promoting his own career at the expense of the striking players would cause nothing but trouble. "You'd have an 'X' on your back for the rest of your career if you did that," he stated.

Jeter hoped his good year in 1994 would earn him a spot as a starter on the Yankees roster for 1995. But the Yankees decided to go with experience and signed veteran shortstop Tony Fernandez to a two-year contract. Jeter took the news in stride. "I've still got more steps to make and the strike stopped that step last season," he said. "It'll work out."

Unexpected Call

When the 1995 season was little more than a month old, however, Jeter got a call from the Yankees. Tony Fernandez was injured and on the disabled list, and they needed Jeter to report to Seattle immediately. He called his family with the news. "Dad, I'm out of here," he said. Though it was wonderful news, it presented a problem for Jeter's parents. Their daughter Sharlee was the star shortstop on the Kalamazoo Central softball team, and she would be playing in an important tournament game the same day that their son would start his major league career. With typical fair-mindedness, they decided that Dorothy would stay home to cheer on Sharlee while Charles flew to Seattle to watch Derek's first Yankee game.

Jeter failed to get a hit in his first major league game, but he was flawless on defense. In the eighth inning, he dove and stopped a single from becoming an extra-base hit, preserving a tie. The next night he had two hits and scored two runs. Jeter played 13 games for the Yankees, until Fernandez returned from the disabled list. During that time he batted .234 and drove in six runs. "I can control how I play and so far I'm doing okay, but I could be doing better," he admitted. Jeter then returned to the AAA team in Columbus. He returned to the Yankees briefly in September, but he had only one time at bat, in which he hit a double. Jeter says he actually learned more by sitting on the bench in September than by playing in June. "The second time around I saw everything, because I *didn't* play," he says.

To improve his skills, Jeter went back to the Yankee training complex in Tampa immediately after the 1995 season. "I was at the complex every day," he remembered. During that winter, the Yankees top management decided that Jeter had spent enough time in the minor leagues. "Derek Jeter is going to be our shortstop going in [to the 1996 season]," announced Joe Torre, the new manager.

Major League Rookie Season

On the opening day of the 1996 season in a game against the Cleveland Indians, Jeter hit a home run, and the Yankees won. The next week, at the home opener in New York, Jeter hit another home run, and the Yankees won again. It turned out to be a dream season for the young shortstop. He ended the year batting .314 to become the first Yankees shortstop in 40 years to hit above .300 for a full season. He also had a 17-game hitting streak, the longest for a rookie since Joe DiMaggio's 18 games in 1936. His 78 RBIs were the highest for a rookie shortstop since 1980, and his 183 hits led the Yankees. With his help, the Yankees won the American League East title for the first time in 15 years.

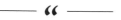

Jeter is the first player to win three world championships by age 25 since divisional play began in 1969.
"He's played his whole career in the World Series,"
said teammate Chili Davis.
"I've just been very fortunate to be on good teams," Jeter claims.

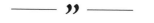

The Yankees defeated Texas in the division series, three games to one. Then, in the American League Championship Series against Baltimore, Jeter was involved in a play that is still remembered and talked about. The Orioles were leading in the eighth inning, 4-3, when Jeter came to bat. He hit a long fly ball to right, and Oriole right fielder Tony Tarasco went back to the warning track and waited for it. But before the ball landed in his glove, a 12-year-old boy reached out and caught it. Tarasco pointed angrily at the boy, but umpire Rich Garcia signaled a home run. "I thought the ball was going out of the ballpark," Garcia explained. "I really didn't feel that Tarasco was going to catch the ball, so I called it a home run." Tarasco couldn't believe it. "It was like magic," he said afterward. "I was about to catch the ball, and it disappeared." The Oriole manager, Davey Johnson, was ejected from the game for arguing. The Yankees went on to win the game. Four games later, they captured the League Championship Series and earned a place in the World Series.

In the World Series, the Yankees beat the Atlanta Braves in six games. Jeter's 22 hits set a new record for hits by a rookie in postseason play. His amazing season made him the unanimous choice for American League Rookie of the Year by the Baseball Writers Association of America. The

Jeter is surrounded by teammates as they celebrate after defeating the Cleveland Indians, 9-5, in Game 6 of the American League Championship Series, October 13, 1998.

Black Baseball Writers Association of America also named him the winner of the Jackie Robinson Rookie of the Year award.

Many athletes struggle after a great rookie year. In some cases, opponents have an opportunity to analyze the new player and figure out his weaknesses. Often there is just a natural tendency to ease back a bit. But though his batting average slipped slightly from .314 to .297, Jeter proved his rookie year was no fluke. In 1997, he reduced his fielding errors from 22 to 18. He also increased his walks from 48 to 74, showing that he had become more selective at the plate. The Yankees made the division series as the wild card team, but lost the series to the Cleveland Indians.

Probably the biggest challenge for Jeter in his second major league season was learning to cope with being a celebrity. He had gotten a taste of the media spotlight in 1996, but to his surprise he was now idolized, especially by female fans. *People Magazine* included him in its list of the 50 Most Beautiful People in the World. Huge crowds of girls and young women waited for him before and after games and everywhere else he was due to appear, screaming everything from autograph requests to marriage proposals. "In terms of the girls screaming all the time," Jeter joked, "everybody else [on the team] is married, so they're pretty much stuck with me."

At about this time Jeter started dating singer Mariah Carey. To his dismay, he discovered that reporters would follow them everywhere, often writing stories that were not true or exaggerated. Opposing teams played Mariah Carey songs when he stepped up to bat, and fans held up signs with their names inside a heart. This kind of constant intrusion into their private lives caused the two to stop dating. "It's bad enough when one public person is involved. But with two, it's really hard to have something to yourself," Carey explained. For Jeter, it was a lesson that public attention can be hard to take.

> *Jeter downplays comparisons to baseball greats Pete Rose and Ty Cobb, saying "I think it's unfair to them for me to be compared to them. Those were great, great players who played for many years and accomplished many great things." Jeter does have at least one long-term goal, though. "I want to win 11 championships," he says with a smile.*

By the start of the 1998 season people thought they had seen Jeter at his best. He was viewed as a dependable, solid .300 hitter and a decent fielder—an all-around good player. But Jeter continued to improve.

In 1998, Jeter increased his hit total from 190 to 203, his home runs from 10 to 19, and his batting average from .291 to .324. His 127 runs scored led the league. The Yankees won 114 games, which was the second-best record in baseball history, then barreled through the playoffs and swept the World Series in four games. At the celebration in New York, Jeter was awarded the key to the city. "I don't think there's a person in the world who's been more spoiled than I've been," he said modestly.

Great as these numbers were, Jeter improved on them yet again in 1999, batting .349 with 219 hits and 24 home runs. He won a Gold Glove Award for his fielding and finished second in the race for the batting title. He broke the major league record for most runs scored by a shortstop in his first three full seasons. The Yankees again won the World Series, mak-

Jeter kicks off Jeter's Leadership Program, in Kalamazoo, MI, January 26, 2000.

ing Jeter the first player to win three world championships by age 25 since divisional play began in 1969. "He's played his whole career in the World Series," said teammate Chili Davis. "I've just been very fortunate to be on good teams," Jeter explained.

As the 2000 baseball season got underway, people were comparing Jeter to some of the greatest players in the game. For example, his name is often mentioned along with Pete Rose and Ty Cobb, who rank first and second for career hits. In his first four years in pro ball, Jeter has more hits than either of those players for the same time period. If he continues on his current pace for 15 years, he will end up with more than 4,000 hits. (Rose had 4,256 and Cobb 4,189.) Jeter downplays such comparisons, saying "I think it's unfair to them [Rose and Cobb] for me to be compared to them. Those were great, great players who played for many years and accomplished many great things." Jeter does have at least one long-term goal, though. "I want to win 11 championships," he says with a smile.

HOME AND FAMILY

Jeter has a home in Tampa, Florida, near the Yankees training complex. During the baseball season, he rents an apartment on the Upper East Side of Manhattan, a borough of New York City. He is very happy with his location. "If you're looking for complaints, I don't have any," he stated.

51

"OK, traffic here is a pain, but other than that, I'm living in a dream." He remains close to his parents and sister. Though he occasionally dates, Jeter has become wary of getting seriously involved with anyone. "It's hard for me to have a relationship the way things are right now," he admitted. "I'd have to be with someone very understanding, someone who's willing to deal with all the attention."

HOBBIES AND OTHER INTERESTS

When asked about his hobbies, Jeter answers, "Movies and sleeping. Those are my hobbies." He tends to avoid nights out on the town with large groups of people. "I don't really go out," he explained. "Basically what I do every night, even in the off-season, [is] dinner and a movie. I eat all the time and watch so many movies that I could be a movie critic." He likes the kind of rolled-over pizza that is available in New York, along with chicken parmesan. His favorite music is rhythm and blues, and hip-hop. Not surprisingly, Mariah Carey is his favorite singer.

Jeter also takes an active interest in the Turn 2 Foundation, which he established in 1996. "The support for the foundation is just great," Jeter says enthusiastically. "I wanted to give back to the community, and this is a great way to do it."

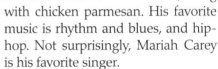

Jeter also takes an active interest in the Turn 2 Foundation, which he established in 1996. "As a kid, I was a big Dave Winfield fan," he noted. "I always said that if and when I ever made it I wanted to be like him and have my own foundation." The foundation, managed by his father, raises money for college scholarships and programs that help kids stay away from drugs and alcohol. Turn 2 (2 is the number on Jeter's Yankee uniform) has provided funds for the Boys and Girls Club of New York, the Phoenix Academy, and the YMCA Black Achiever Program in Michigan. So far it has raised more than $500,000. "The support for the foundation is just great," Jeter says enthusiastically. "I wanted to give back to the community, and this is a great way to do it."

In January 2000, Jeter started a new program, Jeter's Leadership Program, which he announced from his hometown of Kalamazoo. The program supports students committed to excellence and to an alcohol- and drug-free lifestyle. He was joined in announcing the program with several professional athletes who will act as role models for students all over the country.

Jeter has also begun to take classes in the off-season at the University of Michigan. It will probably take him several years, but he's determined to get a college degree.

HONORS AND AWARDS

High School Player of the Year (American Baseball Coaches
    Association): 1992
Minor-League Player of the Year (*Baseball America*): 1994
Minor League Player of the Year (*Sporting News*): 1994
Minor League Player of the Year (*USA Today*): 1994
American League Rookie of the Year: 1996
American League All-Star: 1998, 1999
Gold Glove Award: 1999

FURTHER READING

Books

Craig, Robert. *Derek Jeter: A Biography*, 1999 (juvenile)
Giles, Patrick. *Derek Jeter: Pride of the Yankees*, 1998
O'Connell, Jack. *Derek Jeter: The Yankee Kid*, 1999 (juvenile)
Stewart, Mark. *Derek Jeter: Substance and Style*, 1999 (juvenile)
Who's Who in America, 2000

Periodicals

Chicago Tribune, July 29, 1999
Detroit Free Press, May 27, 1992, p.D1; June 29, 1999, p.D1; July 6, 1999,
    p.C2
Ebony, July 1999, p.68; Apr. 2000, p.148
Gentleman's Quarterly, Feb. 1998, p.138; Sep. 1998, p.356
New York, Apr. 7, 1997, p.24
New York Post, Mar. 31, 1999, p.46
New York Times, Apr. 4, 1999, sec. 8, p.1; Mar. 12, 2000, p. A33
Newsday, Aug. 18, 1994, p.A82; Mar. 3, 1996, Sports sec., p.13; Sep. 30,
    1996, Playoffs sec., p.5; Mar. 16, 1997, p.B16
Sports Illustrated, May 6, 1996, p.44; Feb. 24, 1997, p.50; June 21, 1999,
    p.100

Sports Illustrated for Kids, July 1998, p.34
USA Today, June 25, 1992, p.C8; Oct. 15, 1996, p.C6; Oct. 26, 1999, p.C1
Washington Post, Feb. 22, 1997, p.B1

ADDRESS

New York Yankees
Yankee Stadium
161 1st and River Ave.
Bronx, NY 10341

WORLD WIDE WEB SITES

http://espn.go.com/mlb
http://www.majorleaguebaseball.com

Karch Kiraly 1960-

American Professional Volleyball Player
Three-Time Olympic Gold Medalist in Indoor and
Beach Volleyball

BIRTH

Charles Frederick Kiraly (pronounced KEER-eye) was born on
November 3, 1960, in Jackson, Michigan. His mother, Toni
(Iffland) Kiraly, worked as a librarian, elementary school
teacher, and real estate agent. His father, Laszlo Kiraly, was a
doctor who specialized in physical rehabilitation. An immi-
grant from Hungary, Laszlo had been forced to flee to the

United States in 1956, when the Soviet Union invaded his homeland. He still retained great pride in his ethnic heritage, though, and he nicknamed his son Karczi (KARCH-ee), which is a rough Hungarian version of Charles. Friends eventually shortened this nickname to "Karch," the name he goes by today. Karch grew up with two younger sisters, Kati and Kristi.

YOUTH

Kiraly spent his early childhood years in Ann Arbor, Michigan, while his father attended medical school at the University of Michigan. "I was a happy kid in Ann Arbor, in Little League and Boy Scouts, and playing with my friends," Kiraly remembers. He credits both of his parents with helping him flourish during these early years. His mother watched over him with great patience and love, while his father instilled in him a hardy work ethic and sense of responsibility. "I grew up in a pretty disciplined household," he said. "I think it was that old-world ethic, where instead of complaining a lot about your problems you just work harder to make them better."

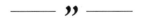

"We played so much and got so good so fast. To see ourselves improving almost daily, spending our summers doing what we loved to do, was a dream. Plus, playing all those hours in the sand gave us legs of steel and did wonders for our body control."

In 1971 the Kiraly family moved west to California, eventually settling in Santa Barbara in 1974. When his family first moved to California, young Karch's favorite sport was soccer. But he soon became intrigued with beach volleyball, a game that was popular on beaches all up and down the California coastline. His father loved the California volleyball scene as well. He had been a member of Hungary's Junior National volleyball team before immigrating to the United States. Before long, Karch was spending many of his afternoons at area beaches, watching his father compete in regional tournaments.

At age 11, Kiraly began playing in two-man beach tournaments with his father. These matches were very difficult for young Kiraly. Opposing teams — most of whom consisted of older players in their late teens and early twenties — mercilessly focused on the young player's weaknesses. They drilled him with hard spikes and forced him to run all over the court. Kiraly's father sometimes lost his temper when his son struggled, even though he knew that Karch was doing his best. "I pushed him very hard in those days," Laszlo Kiraly admitted. "I was critical of him. I could see him seething inside. I forgot that he was 11 or 12 years old."

But despite these early knocks, Kiraly gritted his teeth and refused to quit. He found other kids his age who shared his enthusiasm for the sport, and they spent countless days down at the local beach. On many days, they played two-on-two—the standard set-up for competitive beach volley-ball—from dawn until dusk. Before long, Kiraly and his buddies found themselves moving steadily up through the ranks of local players. "We played so much and got so good so fast," he recalled. "To see ourselves improving almost daily, spending our summers doing what we loved to do, was a dream. Plus, playing all those hours in the sand gave us legs of steel and did wonders for our body control." It also made him even better at indoor volleyball, in which six-player teams compete against one another.

EDUCATION

Kiraly attended the public schools in Ann Arbor and Santa Barbara. He went to Santa Barbara High School, where he excelled both on the volley-ball court and in the classroom. He graduated third in a class of 800 students with a 3.96 grade point average (GPA). During his senior year, meanwhile, he led his high school volleyball team to an unbeaten record and regional championship. Even at this early age, Kiraly's instincts for the game were superior to those of other players his age. But the biggest weapon at his disposal was his incredible jumping ability, which made him a very dangerous spiker. "Karch was a scrawny kid," recalled his high school coach. "But he had the biggest calves. Standing under the basket *on one leg,* he could jump up and stuff a volleyball. The basketball team would watch in amazement."

In the summer of 1977, Kiraly became the youngest player ever to earn a spot on America's Junior National Team. This indoor volleyball team gathered top players under age 21 from across the United States to play other squads from around the world. The 16-year-old Kiraly did not get to play very much, but he received valuable experience practicing against some of America's finest college players. In addition, his membership on the team gave him the opportunity to visit distant cities like Honolulu, Hawaii, and Sao Paulo, Brazil. When the season ended, Kiraly promptly returned to the beach to play sand volleyball.

Not surprisingly, Kiraly says that volleyball dominated his high school years. "I imagine I was seen by most of my peers as a volleyball jock who got good grades," he said. "Most of my friends were guys on the volleyball team. . . . Certainly I wasn't one of the coolest guys in school. Clothes weren't an issue for me and never have been. . . . To this day, my preferred attire is shorts and a T-shirt."

After graduating from Santa Barbara High in 1979, Kiraly weighed volleyball scholarship offers from several West Coast schools. He eventually decided to attend UCLA (University of California-Los Angeles), which had one of the strongest programs in the country. Upon arriving at UCLA, Kiraly proved that his high school grades were no fluke. In fact, he graduated from the school in 1983 with a 3.55 GPA and a bachelor's degree in biochemistry. But his most visible triumphs at UCLA took place on the volleyball court.

> "I imagine I was seen by most of my peers as a volleyball jock who got good grades. Most of my friends were guys on the volleyball team. . . . Certainly I wasn't one of the coolest guys in school. Clothes weren't an issue for me and never have been. . . . To this day, my preferred attire is shorts and a T-shirt."

CAREER HIGHLIGHTS

A Rising Star—Both Inside and on the Beach

Kiraly enjoyed a spectacular volleyball career with the UCLA Bruins. During his four years at the school, the squad became a nearly unstoppable machine. The Bruins won 124 out of 129 matches and three national championships during Kiraly's college career. During this time, he became known as the best college player in the country. Unfortunately, he also became known—at least among some of his college peers—as a heavy drinker. Kiraly eventually learned to curb his partying ways, but he still looks back on those days with regret. "I don't know why, but some of us at UCLA were pretty out of control—a lot of volleyball parties and a lot of beer drinking," he recalled. "I can't believe how stupid and destructive that behavior was, and what a poor example I set. At least I figured it out—some people never do."

Kiraly's growth into a dominating hardcourt (indoor) player paralleled his increasing skill at the sand game. In fact, Kiraly and teammate Sinjin Smith emerged as the best sand team in the country during the summers of 1979 and 1980. They won nearly every tournament they entered, easily trouncing most of the teams they played. But in 1981, Kiraly was forced to make a very tough choice between indoor volleyball and the beach game that he had grown up playing.

Team USA

In the summer of 1981, Kiraly joined the Team USA, America's national indoor team and the team that would represent the U.S. in the 1984 Olympics. He became an immediate starter on the squad, which played in international competitions around the world. But Kiraly's membership on the team forced him to set sand volleyball aside for the next few years. Team USA head coach Doug Beal feared that his players might get injured or de-

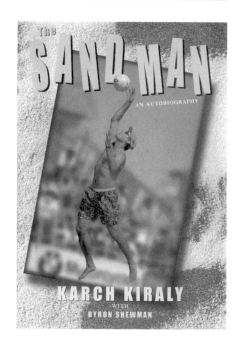

velop bad habits if they played sand ball. As a result, he handed down a rule that forbade team members from playing in beach tournaments. Kiraly managed to play in a few tournaments anyway, in defiance of Beal's order. But it was hard to enter sand tournaments without Beal's knowledge, and Team USA's full practice and game schedule took up a lot of Kiraly's time. "I would miss many beach seasons because of my indoor career," he recalled. "Beal's decision rankled me, but I had already decided that the Olympic dream was what I wanted most."

During the early 1980s, Team USA emerged as an international power. The addition of Kiraly and several other young stars made the squad a supremely athletic and powerful one. Some observers even said that the Americans might soon be able to challenge the Soviet Union squad, widely regarded as the world's best.

In early 1984, only months before the Summer Olympics in Los Angeles, Team USA traveled to the Soviet Union for a big pre-Olympic match. The clash was widely viewed as a preview of the likely gold medal showdown in Los Angeles, which would be the first Olympics to feature volleyball as a medal-event. The Americans won in a dramatic five-game match, only to learn later in the evening that the Soviets were going to boycott the 1984 Olympic Games because of political differences with the United States.

Olympic Gold and World Cup Championships

The absence of the Soviet Union from the 1984 Games disappointed Kiraly and his teammates. They wanted to earn gold by beating the best that the world had to offer. But once they arrived in Los Angeles, Team USA shook off the disappointment and took special care to avoid a mental letdown. They cruised through the early rounds, then defeated Brazil in three straight games to take gold medal honors. "My feet didn't touch the ground for the next two months," Kiraly said. "That first [gold medal] in L.A. was such a thrill because we were playing at home, and we'd won the first [Olympic] gold medal ever in our sport."

A year later, Team USA resumed its rivalry with the Soviet squad in the World Cup, one of three "Triple Crown" events that are the most prestigious in volleyball (the other two are the Olympics and the World Championships). As it turned out, the whole tournament hinged on the second-round match between the two powerhouses. "It was phenomenal," Kiraly remembered. "We beat the Soviets in . . . one of the longest [games] ever played. It took 3 hours, 36 minutes, and my dad, who was there, said he lived about five years before we were done. We played a best-of-five-game match, and in the fifth game we were down 9-3, 10-4, and 11-5 before we came back to win 15-12. We outscored them 10-1 to win." When the Americans clinched the victory, Kiraly admitted that "we went nuts. In many ways it was even bigger than the Olympics because we had finally knocked the Soviets off their perch in a Triple Crown event—something the USA had never done."

Team USA maintained its top-dog status in international volleyball for the next few seasons. In 1986 it won the World Championships. A year later, the USA squad captured a gold medal in the Pan-American Games. Since Kiraly was recognized as America's best player, these victories dramatically increased his fame in volleyball-crazy countries like Japan and Brazil. In fact, he was often mobbed when he walked the streets in those nations. In America, on the other hand, Kiraly remained largely unknown outside of volleyball circles.

Back to Beach Volleyball

In 1985, Marv Dunphy took over head coaching duties on Team USA. Unlike Beal, he did not mind if his players competed in sand tournaments in their free time. This policy change thrilled Kiraly. He missed playing in the sand, and he knew that the beach game had developed into a much more organized and successful sport during the early 1980s. This growth was widely credited to the Association of Volleyball Professionals (AVP), which organized tours all across the country after its formation in 1983. As Kiraly stated, "The AVP was really starting to take off and I wanted to be a part of it, both for the money and the fun."

But Kiraly's return to beach volleyball turned out to be a frustrating experience. He found that it was very difficult to find a good playing partner, since he could only compete in about half of the sand events. "Even with Dunphy allowing me to play when I had free weekends, it still wasn't enough," he stated. "The very top players wanted to stay with the same partner for an entire season. . . . My indoor obligations scared away the best players." Forced to play with ever-changing partners, Kiraly had only limited success during his first summer on the pro beach circuit.

The 1988 Olympics

As the 1988 Olympic Games approached, many volleyball experts believed that the United States men's team had a good chance to grab a second straight gold medal. This belief was due in large part to the continued presence of Kiraly on the team. "He's the most complete volleyball player in the world," said Beal. "I don't know if Wayne Gretzky is the greatest athlete who ever skated, but I bet he is the best player. That's the way I view Karch. He combines all the skills better than anyone else." Dunphy, who coached the 1988 Olympic team, agreed: "Karch was the best indoor player ever, and I say that without any hesitation. He had the body, the physical skills, the mental makeup, the total package. And you know, I don't think I ever once did anything to motivate Karch."

"He's the most complete volleyball player in the world," said Olympic coach Doug Beal. "I don't know if Wayne Gretzky is the greatest athlete who ever skated, but I bet he is the best player. That's the way I view Karch. He combines all the skills better than anyone else."

Kiraly's skills were on full display at the 1988 Olympics in Seoul, South Korea. Team USA won another gold medal, defeating the Soviet Union in the final. They were led by Kiraly, who put on an amazing display of powerful spikes, pinpoint passing, and tough defense throughout the competition. He was rewarded for his performance with the tournament's Most Valuable Player award.

Kiraly returns the ball during the 1988 Olympics.

Kiraly was very happy to earn a second gold medal. But he later confessed that he felt more relieved than anything. "I had stressed so hard for those two weeks in Seoul that . . . I was entirely spent [afterward]. I didn't have enough energy to go to the closing ceremonies. I had nothing left. I got together with Janna [his wife] and our family at a . . . reception and we kicked back with a couple of big Cokes. No big celebration like in 1984. I was simply too exhausted."

A Legend in the Sand

After the 1988 Olympics, Kiraly left Team USA. He played in professional leagues in Italy in both 1990 and 1991. He received a generous salary for his services during that time, but by the end of the second season he was ready to move his family back to the United States. "How ecstatic we were when we finally got home!" Kiraly recalled. "We had learned that the best way to appreciate how fortunate we are in America is to live elsewhere for a while."

Upon returning to the U.S., Kiraly decided to focus all his energy on beach volleyball. He even turned down an invitation to play for Team USA in the 1992 Summer Olympics in Barcelona, Spain. "I really felt like I would regret never accomplishing my goals on the beach, or missing special moments with my kids, more than I would miss winning a third gold medal," he explained. "By 1992 I was dying to get back to where I played my first game at age nine. I'd been away long enough from the sun, the sand, the ocean, the California dream I loved so much. I now had a wife and two young sons, and a house in San Clemente. Tired of the nonstop traveling and playing in hundreds of gyms around the world, I was ready for the beach. So was my family."

> " *"By 1992 I was dying to get back to where I played my first game at age nine. I'd been away long enough from the sun, the sand, the ocean, the California dream I loved so much. I now had a wife and two young sons, and a house in San Clemente. Tired of the nonstop traveling and playing in hundreds of gyms around the world, I was ready for the beach. So was my family."* "

As the 1992 beach season approached, Kiraly joined forces with Kent Steffes, a powerful and talented young player. The partnership turned out to be a formidable one. The Kiraly-Steffes team won 16 of the last 19 tournaments in which they competed that summer, including 13 victories in a row. Their spectacular success convinced Kiraly that his decision to pass on the 1992 Olympics had been the correct one. "If I had played in the Olympics, Kent and I would not have accomplished what now is considered the best season anyone ever had in beach volleyball," he said.

As it turned out, the 1992 season marked only the beginning of a multi-year stretch of dominance for the Kiraly-Steffes team. In 1993, the duo claimed 19 victories in 25 events. A year later, they registered 17 wins in 22 tournaments. And in both 1995 and 1996, they won at least half of the tournaments they entered. Many of their victories during this five-year stretch were major beach championships.

During this same period, beach volleyball surged in popularity all across the United States. Thousands of new fans flocked to the tournaments every month, lured by the game's summer beach party atmosphere and hip reputation. Tournament purses increased as a result, and Kiraly became the first beach player in history to surpass $2 million in career earnings.

Kiraly also emerged as the best-known player in the country during this time. His name became synonymous with beach volleyball among fans and players alike. No other player could duplicate his steady brilliance in the sand or his glorious record as an indoor player. By the mid-1990s, many people felt that he had become the greatest player in the history of the sport. "You can't compare Karch to other volleyball players anymore," said one fellow beach player. "You have to compare him with guys like Michael Jordan, because he's not only the most dominating volleyball player, but one of the greatest athletes ever."

Return to the Olympics — 1996

When Kiraly turned down an invitation to participate in the 1992 Olympics, he didn't know he would get another opportunity to win a third gold medal. But when organizers of the 1996 Games in Atlanta, Georgia, made beach volleyball a medal sport for the first time, Kiraly saw his chance.

In the months leading up to the 1996 Summer Olympics, Kiraly and Steffes trained harder than ever before. Their dedication paid off in Olympic glory, as they defeated fellow Americans Mike Dodd and Mike Whitmarsh to claim the gold. Their 12-5, 12-8 victory established Kiraly as the first American ever to win three gold medals in Olympic volleyball competition. "I'm very happy for Karch and Kent," Whitmarsh said after the match. "They've been the dominant team for four or five years. If you lose, you want to lose to the best. Besides, Karch Kiraly has done more for volleyball than anyone I know."

Kiraly returns the ball against fellow countrymen Mike Dodd and Mike Whitmarsh during their beach volleyball game at the Olympics in Atlanta, July 28, 1996.

Kent Steffes, left, wipes his eyes as Kiraly salutes the flag after winning the gold medal in the men's beach volleyball finals of the 1996 Olympics.

Kiraly says that the 1996 triumph was especially sweet because it featured two American teams that respected one another. "When the last ball touched the ground, I tackled Kent in jubilation," Kiraly recalled. "We got to our feet and ran to the net where the four of us had a group hug and congratulated each other. That moment was special for me in a different sense, compared with my other two Olympic finals. Here were four guys who had played so hard and done so much to get to this ultimate moment — for themselves and for their sport. Four buddies. Four beach volleyball players."

A Serious Injury and a Struggling League

Kiraly's career took a sudden downturn in the months following his 1996 Olympic triumph. A few weeks after competing in Atlanta, he tore the rotator cuff in his right shoulder. "Through use and abuse in 29 years of volleyball, it finally gave way," he said. The injury required major surgery and extensive rehabilitation. In the meantime, Steffes left Kiraly for another partner, ending a six-year relationship. Kiraly was disappointed to see their partnership end, but he insisted that there were no hard feelings. "It's an inevitability in this game, especially if you have more than a year or two age difference between you and your partner," he said. "I understand Kent's decision. If I was in his position, I probably would have done the same thing."

Kiraly struggled to regain his pre-injury form in 1997. At the same time, he reluctantly agreed to requests that he join the AVP's Board of Directors. Within months of Kiraly's joining, however, the organization was rocked by disclosures of major financial and administrative problems. "The financial records were a total mess, as were most other aspects of the business, including legal and administrative," Kiraly said.

The AVP's internal problems soon triggered a bitter battle among the sport's players and officials. At times, the disputes threatened to tear the sport apart. At one point, Kiralys' former partner Steffes even filed a lawsuit against Kiraly and other AVP directors over lost prize money. This legal action effectively destroyed the relationship between the two star players. The AVP, meanwhile, was reorganized under new management in 1999.

—— " ——

Kiraly says that the 1996 triumph was especially sweet because it featured two American teams that respected one another. "When the last ball touched the ground, I tackled Kent in jubilation. We got to our feet and ran to the net where the four of us had a group hug and congratulated each other. That moment was special for me in a different sense, compared with my other two Olympic finals. Here were four guys who had played so hard and done so much to get to this ultimate moment — for themselves and for their sport. Four buddies. Four beach volleyball players."

—— " ——

Still a Threat

It took Kiraly months to fully recover from the rotator cuff injury. In 1997 he and his partners managed only four tournament victories. By the end of that summer, some people thought that Kiraly—who by that time was several years older than nearly all of his opponents—was fading as a player.

In 1998, however, Kiraly came roaring back. He won six out of 19 tournaments with new partner Adam Johnson. And in 1999, the Kiraly-Johnson team registered victories in many of the AVP events they entered. By the end of the 1999 season, Kiraly had an amazing 141 career wins.

Kiraly recognizes that he will not be able to play competitive beach volleyball forever. But, he says, "it's still a really fun thing for me to do. I consider myself lucky to be playing beach volleyball and earn a living at it, and as long as I'm having fun, even if I'm not winning anymore, I can see myself playing for quite a number of years."

Another Olympics?

In the spring of 2000, Kiraly made his intentions clear. "Our plans are to definitely make a run for the Olympics," he said of the Kiraly-Johnson team. So as the Olympics of 2000, set to take place in Sydney, Australia, approach, Kiraly could be poised to make a record fourth appearance. Still, he keeps everything in perspective. "We're not going to kill ourselves qualifying," he says. "If it happens, great. If it doesn't' I won't be crying in my milk."

Kiraly recognizes that he will not be able to play competitive beach volleyball forever. But, he says, "it's still a really fun thing for me to do. I consider myself lucky to be playing beach volleyball and earn a living at it, and as long as I'm having fun, even if I'm not winning anymore, I can see myself playing for quite a number of years." He also wants to stay associated with the sport when his playing days do finally end. "My future in the game? I definitely want to stay in it, but I'm not sure what that means. Television broadcasting, clinics, and camps are all strong possibilities. I'm sure I'll eventually do more to help people learn about the game. I'd also like to carve out a niche for myself on the business side of the sport."

MARRIAGE AND FAMILY

Kiraly married Janna Miller in 1986. They have two sons, Kristian and Kory, and live in San Clemente, California. Kiraly says that he often plays volleyball with his boys and their friends. But he insists that he will put no pressure on them to follow in his footsteps. "I only want my kids to play volleyball if it's their own choice. If they pursue other interests, that's fine. There's been enough volleyball in my life to suffice for my entire family. In fact, during much of my life, my commitment to the sport left me too little time for others."

HOBBIES AND OTHER INTERESTS

In his spare time, Kiraly enjoys reading about American history, politics, and other subjects.

WRITINGS

Beach Volleyball, 1999 (with Byron Shewman)
The Sandman: An Autobiography, 1999 (with Byron Shewman)

HONORS AND AWARDS

Player of the Year (California High School Volleyball): 1978
NCAA Men's Volleyball Championship Team: 1979, 1981, 1982
NCAA Scholar-Athlete Award: 1982
Olympic Indoor Volleyball: 1984, Gold Medal; 1988, Gold Medal
Best Player in the World Award (FIVB): 1986, 1988
Pan-Am Games: 1987, Gold Medal
Most Valuable Player (Association of Volleyball Professionals): 1990, 1992, 1993, 1994, 1995, 1998, 1999
Sportsman of the Year (Association of Volleyball Professionals): 1995, 1997
Olympic Beach Volleyball: 1996, Gold Medal
Comeback Player of the Year (Association of Volleyball Professionals): 1997

FURTHER READING

Books

Kiraly, Karch. *The Sandman: An Autobiography,* 1999 (with Byron Shewman)
Shewman, Byron. *Volleyball Centennial: The First 100 Years,* 1995
Who's Who in America, 2000

Periodicals

Atlanta Journal and Constitution, May 18, 1997, p.F2
Chicago Tribune, July 5, 1999, Section: Sports, p.9
Fort Lauderdale Sun-Sentinel, Apr. 30, 2000, p.C19
Los Angeles Times, Aug. 24, 1988, p.C3; June 30, 1989, p.C3; June 12, 1992,
    p.C12; Aug. 25, 1994, p.C1; Aug. 26, 1995, p.C4
Los Angeles Times Magazine, Feb. 23, 1986, p.18
New York Times, June 14, 1984, p.D24; Feb. 24, 1995, p.B11; July 29, 1996,
    p.C9
Orange County (California) Register, June 10, 1999, p.D17
Palm Beach Post, Apr. 14, 2000, p.C1
Rolling Stone, July 16, 1987, p.87
Sports Illustrated, June 2, 1986, p.71; July 10, 1989, p.24; June 22, 1992, p.34;
    Aug. 5, 1996, p.88
Sports Illustrated for Kids, Feb. 1996, p.799; June 1997, p.62
USA Today, July 8, 1996, p.C12

WORLD WIDE WEB SITE

www.bvbdb.com

Alex Lowe 1958-1999

American Mountain Climber
Made Famous Ascents of Mountains in North
America, Antarctica, Pakistan, Nepal, and Elsewhere

BIRTH

Stewart Alexander Lowe was born on December 24, 1958, in
Missoula, Montana. He grew up in the town of Missoula,
where his father, Jim, worked as a professor of entomology
(the study of insects) at the University of Montana. His moth-

er, Dorothea, worked as a schoolteacher in Missoula. Lowe had two brothers, Andy, who is older, and Ted, who is younger.

YOUTH

Lowe was an intensely curious and energetic youngster. "Alex was one of those little kids who never felt tame," recalled his mother. "He always had trouble sitting still." Fortunately for young Lowe, he was part of a family that shared his adventurous and active spirit. In fact, Lowe's parents loved nothing more than to disappear into the nearby mountains for days at a time on extended camping trips. "We didn't pack up the station wagon and go to Disneyland," remembered Lowe. "We packed our backpacks and went off to the Beartooth Mountains or the Missions or the Bob Marshall Wilderness. I just have all these great memories of growing up as a little kid with a big backpack on my back, trying to keep up with my dad and my mom and my brothers."

> *"We didn't pack up the station wagon and go to Disneyland. We packed our backpacks and went off to the Beartooth Mountains or the Missions or the Bob Marshall Wilderness. I just have all these great memories of growing up as a little kid with a big backpack on my back, trying to keep up with my dad and my mom and my brothers."*

It was during these rugged backpacking expeditions that Lowe first developed a taste for rock climbing. "My dad did a little scrambling [hiking over difficult and rocky terrain]," he recalled, "so we'd set up camp at a mountain lake, fish for the evening, and the next day we'd sort of scramble up a peak. For some reason, I really liked that."

By the time he was a teenager, Lowe's fascination with climbing had grown into a full-blown passion. At first, he could not find many other people who shared his excitement, because climbing was not a very popular sport at the time. But over the years, Lowe became part of a small network of other climbers who enjoyed the mountains as much as he did. From that point forward, Lowe and his teenage climbing partners spent most of their summers and after-school time clambering up and down the sides of nearby mountain faces.

EDUCATION

Lowe received his elementary and high school education in the Missoula public schools. A good student, he developed a great interest in mathematics as a teenager. Before long, he showed an ability to approach advanced math problems with the same concentration that he showed when tackling difficult climbing routes.

Lowe graduated from high school in 1977. He then enrolled in Montana State University in Bozeman in the fall of 1977 on a prestigious chemical engineering scholarship. Lowe performed well in his classes, but he remained obsessed with climbing. In fact, his passion for the mountains was so strong that he dropped out of school at the end of his sophomore year and headed for Yosemite National Park in California, home to many of America's most famous climbing areas. "I had the [climbing] bug real bad," Lowe later admitted.

Lowe spent the next few years satisfying his passion for mountain climbing. But he eventually returned to college to continue his education. In 1983 he enrolled again at Montana State University, where he earned a degree in applied mathematics.

CAREER HIGHLIGHTS

Exploring the World

The early 1980s proved to be an exciting and romantic period in Lowe's life. Several months after arriving in Yosemite in 1979, he met Jennifer Leigh, another top climber. A romance quickly blossomed between the two athletes. At the same time, Lowe continued to pursue his love for mountaineering. In fact, he roamed from the Canadian Rockies to the French Alps during this time, always searching for new climbing challenges. He supported himself financially during this time by working as a laborer in the Wyoming oil fields.

In 1982 Lowe and Leigh traveled to the mountains of Europe, where they spent several months climbing. "It's amazing how vivid those memories are," Lowe recalled of that summer. "Climbing was so vibrant and new, plus I was falling in love with Jennifer. I remember climbing all day on the granite sea cliffs near Penzance. The wild appeal: surf crashing at the base of the cliffs, seagulls crying around you."

The couple returned to the United States in late 1982, and they married the following spring. Around this time, Lowe found a job as a mountain climbing guide in Wyoming's Grand Teton range. It was in these mountains that Lowe's legendary abilities as a mountain climber first caught the attention of the international climbing community. In 1984, Lowe and his friend Jack Tackle made the first-ever winter ascent of the north face of the Grand Teton mountain. Then, a few years later, Lowe completed a climbing route known as the Grand Traverse in record time.

The Grand Traverse is a mountaineering route that calls on climbers to ascend 10 different peaks as it winds through the Grand Teton range. Many of America's strongest climbers require at least 24 hours to complete the route, and in the mid-1980s the record time for completing it was 20 hours. Lowe bettered that record by an amazing 11 hours. "He came in [to the guide shop] one morning," recalled a fellow climbing guide. "When he found there wasn't any work that day, he took off in his tennis shoes and did the whole traverse by himself, climbing 10 peaks. He was back by four that afternoon."

A Popular Climbing Partner

In the late 1980s Lowe's reputation continued to grow. He executed amazing ice climbs on frozen waterfalls and mountainsides throughout Montana and Wyoming. He also established more than a dozen new climbing routes on El Capitan, a towering rock wall in Yosemite that ranks as one of the most famous climbing destinations in the world. And in 1989 he made his first major ascent in the Himalayas, taking a never-before-attempted route to the top of Kwangde Nup mountain in Nepal.

In 1990 Lowe and his wife had the first of their three children. Determined to provide his family with good financial security, Lowe accepted a job in Salt Lake City as quality-assurance manager for a climbing and ski gear company. But even though his work responsibilities required him to put in regular office hours, he still found time to indulge his life-long love for the outdoors. He quickly organized a group of fellow outdoor enthusiasts known as the "Dawn Patrol." This collection of mountaineers and skiers regularly gathered together at two or three in the morning to ski or climb in the pre-dawn hours. They would play in the mountains outside the city until daylight, then rush to work with the other Salt Lake City commuters who had slept the night away.

By this time, Lowe had established a significant reputation in mountaineering circles as a gifted and knowledgeable climber. Fellow climbers agreed that he possessed a rare and astonishing combination of strength, endurance, and climbing instincts. They also noted that he was excellent at all kinds of climbing disciplines, including both rock and ice mountaineering and winter and summer climbs. "We're all at this one level of competition," said Conrad Anker. "And then there's Alex."

Still, Lowe became nearly as well-known among expedition partners for other attributes. "Alex was a tremendously fun guy to be around," said National Geographic photographer Gordon Wilsie. "You might call him the greatest climber in the world . . . but he was also just Alex, a practical joker and raconteur [storyteller] who could make almost anyone seem like a special friend, from the president of the National Geographic Society to a yak driver in Tibet."

Lowe also was known among fellow climbers for his incredible energy and enthusiasm. Climber Jack Tackle recalled that when he was in Lowe's company, "I always felt I was standing still next to someone who was running a thousand miles an hour." But Tackle and his fellow mountaineers loved climbing with Lowe anyway. "He was completely uncompetitive to climb with," said one top climber. "He had no ego. It wasn't his personality. He just loved being in the mountains and having fun and pushing himself." Another Montana friend offered a similar assessment. "It was like Michael Jordan calling you up to shoot hoops. He loved the game so much it didn't matter how good or bad you were, only that you were playing with him."

Fellow climbers agreed that Lowe possessed a rare and astonishing combination of strength, endurance, and climbing instincts. They also noted that he was excellent at all kinds of climbing disciplines, including both rock and ice mountaineering and winter and summer climbs. "We're all at this one level of competition," said Conrad Anker. "And then there's Alex."

Mount Everest and Khan Tengri

Lowe's employment at the Salt Lake City climbing gear company lasted for about a year. During that time, he realized that he could not satisfy his passion for climbing while simultaneously holding down a full-time office job. He quit and returned to guiding mountaineering parties in the American Rockies. But he still carved out time to go on several major expeditions overseas. These trips cemented his reputation as one of the world's top climbers.

In August 1993 Lowe set out on a special climb with close friend Conrad Anker, the mountaineer who discovered the body of legendary climber George Mallory on Everest in 1999. Lowe and Anker became the first North Americans ever to compete in the Khan Tengri International Speed

Climbing Competition in Kyrgyzstan in Central Asia. Competitors in this elite climbing event on the northern edge of the Himalayan mountains start at a 13,000-foot base camp. From there, they race to see who can be first to ascend and descend Khan Tengri, a 22,950-foot peak that towers into the heavens. When the race began, Lowe scrambled to an early lead. He then increased his lead, even though he was unfamiliar with the climbing route and not fully used to the thin mountain atmosphere. He ended up completing the race hours ahead of any of his challengers. His final time — ten hours and eight minutes — broke the world speed climbing record by an incredible four hours.

Lowe confessed that both visits to Everest were kind of boring for him. He preferred to climb perilous mountain walls and cliffs of ice that had never been conquered before. "I want to climb routes that are remote and technically difficult. Climbing for me is all about solving the magnitude of the problem. The best projects are the ones with big question marks hanging over them."

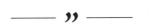

That same year Lowe took part in a successful expedition to the top of Mount Everest, the tallest mountain in the world, located in the Himalayan mountains. A year later, he summited Everest again. But he later confessed that both visits to Everest were kind of boring for him. He preferred to climb perilous mountain walls and cliffs of ice that had never been conquered before. "I want to climb routes that are remote and technically difficult," he explained. "Climbing for me is all about solving the magnitude of the problem. The best projects are the ones with big question marks hanging over them."

The North Face "Dream Team"

In 1995 the North Face mountain equipment company decided to form a "Dream Team" of world-class climbers. Lowe was recruited to join the group, which also included Lynn Hill, Conrad Anker, and Greg Child. Each climber was asked to spend some time reviewing gear and visiting stores that sold North Face equipment. In return, they received generous salaries and the opportunity to spend months at a time on company-sponsored climbing expeditions all around the world. Not surprisingly, Lowe was delighted with the new arrangement. "There's nothing wrong with making money at what I love to do," he said.

Lowe in 1998.

Lowe joined the North Face team at a time when climbing and mountaineering was reaching new heights of popularity in America. Lowe welcomed the increased interest in his sport. "I think that in countries like Switzerland, France, and Italy, mountains are normal to people," said Lowe. "In the United States, mountains are a small part of the country. People in Nebraska and Iowa, they sort of write off all climbers as this fringe element of sort of suicidal characters. But in Europe, climbers are normal. In fact, that's what Swiss families do: they hire a guide and go

———— " ————

"In the United States, mountains are a small part of the country. People in Nebraska and Iowa, they sort of write off all climbers as this fringe element of sort of suicidal characters. But in Europe, climbers are normal. In fact, that's what Swiss families do: they hire a guide and go climbing, generation after generation. Alpinism is a household sport, the way 'normal' sports — you know, basketball and football — are here. Those people are considered the real athletes. But climbing is sort of getting there, it's getting more understood, more accepted in our society. It's just been that way for a lot longer in Europe."

———— " ————

climbing, generation after generation. Alpinism is a household sport, the way 'normal' sports — you know, basketball and football — are here. Those people are considered the real athletes. But climbing is sort of getting there, it's getting more understood, more accepted in our society. It's just been that way for a lot longer in Europe."

Lowe's decision to join North Face made him one of the best-known mountaineers in the world. It also freed him to launch a series of expeditions that underlined his growing reputation as the finest climber of his generation. In June 1995, for instance, Lowe and Lynn Hill made the first-ever free ascent of the forbidding and dangerous 4,000-foot Ak-Su mountain in Kyrgyzstan. A "free ascent" is one in which the climbers do not attach ropes to the mountain in case they fall.

A Daring Rescue

Lowe's most spectacular exploits of 1995 took place on Alaska's Mount McKinley, at 20,320 feet the highest peak in the United States. Lowe and climbing partner Conrad Anker intended to take a challenging route up to the mountain top. Lowe, however, reached their base camp a couple of days before Anker. Impatient to begin climbing, Lowe joined some other climbers who were going to the summit by an easier route. On their way back down, they passed three Spanish climbers who were still working their way up the mountainside.

The next day, a storm swept over the mountain, battering the camp of the Spaniards. Cold and exhausted, they frantically radioed for help. The U.S. Army agreed to send a Chinook helicopter to a landing site 19,500 feet up on the mountain, higher than any Chinook helicopter had ever landed before. The National Park Service, meanwhile, asked Lowe and two other climbers—Mark Twight and Scott Backes—if they would take part in the rescue mission. Lowe and the other mountaineers agreed to help. They ventured out into the storm to the Spaniards' campsite, more than 2,000 feet below the helicopter landing site. "By the time we got to them, one of the Spaniards had already fallen to his death," Lowe recalled. "The other two weren't wearing gloves or hats. They were in the last stages of hypothermia—they were delirious—and their hands were frozen way up past the wrist."

Lowe's two companions took one of the surviving Spaniards with them and started up the mountain to the waiting rescue helicopter. They intended to return to help Lowe with the remaining storm victim, but Lowe decided that the man would die if he waited for Twight and Backes to return. "I stood him up, leaned him against me, and started up," Lowe said. "He just passed out, so I cut a chunk of rope, tied him directly into my harness—he was 20 feet below me—and just started climbing up this thing, dragging the guy. . . . When I reached the fixed ropes [ropes that are attached to the mountain face], I couldn't keep dragging him, but he wouldn't get up. So I finally picked him up, piggyback, and staggered uphill to 19,500 feet and carried him" on to the field where the helicopter was waiting. "It was one of those things you do because you have to do it," Lowe said. The storm-battered climbers then flew to nearby Talkeetna, where the Spanish mountaineers received much-needed medical treatment.

The next day, Lowe returned to Mount McKinley and met Anker at their base camp. But another storm washed over the mountain, trapping a party of Taiwanese climbers at 17,000 feet. When three of the climbers became lost in the storm, the Park Service called on Lowe again. He and Anker made their way through the roaring storm in search of the lost Taiwanese. They were too late to save one of the climbers, but they rescued two other half-frozen survivors.

A Modest Superstar

News of Lowe's rescue efforts at Mount McKinley added to his legendary aura. But people who knew him agree that he never let his fame change him. He remained a modest, friendly, and optimistic man who was tremendously popular with fellow climbers. Even his eccentricities— such as his habit of hauling big calculus textbooks on remote expeditions for pleasure reading—seemed to deepen the affection that the climbing community felt for its greatest star.

Lowe climbing an ice flow in Hyalite Canyon near Bozeman, Montana, early 1999.

For his part, Lowe refused to get caught up in debates about his place in the history of mountaineering. "I sort of steer clear of the whole 'world's best climber' stuff," he said. "It's a sort of hype, really, and climbing just doesn't lend itself to that. There might be a fastest runner, or a highest jumper — you can measure [those skills]. But climbing is different. It's just too subjective." Instead, he continued to live by his often-stated belief that "the best climber is the one who has the most fun." On another occasion, he simply divided all climbers into two groups: "Those who climb because their heart sings when they're in the mountains, and all the rest."

New Challenges on Baffin Island and Antarctica

Lowe continued to divide his time between climbing and family in the late 1990s. He loved spending time with his family at their Bozeman, Montana, home. But his passion for mountaineering remained strong, and he continued to go on extended trips to the far corners of the earth.

In 1997, Lowe led a small climbing expedition to the Queen Maud Land region of Antarctica. Braving temperatures that plunged to minus 40 degrees, the party became the first to successfully summit a dangerous, razor-like peak known as Rakekniven that juts 2,000 feet straight out of the Antarctic ice cap. The group then returned to civilization, but Antarctica's frozen beauty—and its countless unclimbed peaks—left a deep impression on Lowe. "Antarctica has a special sort of tug on my heart strings," he admitted. "It's . . . a place where nothing has happened for a long time and nothing's going to happen for a long time to come. It's just sort of infinite."

> *Lowe refused to get caught up in debates about his place in the history of mountaineering. "I sort of steer clear of the whole 'world's best climber' stuff. It's a sort of hype, really, and climbing just doesn't lend itself to that. There might be a fastest runner, or a highest jumper—you can measure [those skills]. But climbing is different. It's just too subjective." Instead, Lowe continued to live by his often-stated belief that "the best climber is the one who has the most fun." On another occasion, he simply divided all climbers into two groups: "Those who climb because their heart sings when they're in the mountains, and all the rest."*

A year later, Lowe and two other climbers made the first successful summit of Great Sail Peak, an extremely challenging mountain located on Baffin Island in northern Canada. The mountain took several weeks to conquer, but Lowe's trademark energy never waned. Fellow climber Mark Synnott recalled that at one point, they were camped on a ledge at 17,000 feet, waiting out bad weather. "We were all just sitting around," he said, "but Alex had built himself this small gym out of boulders and stuff on the other side of the ledge. He had put up a pullup bar, had bungees to do curls, and built up rocks so he could do dips. He went through camp with his gym shorts on, going tent to tent, asking if anyone wanted to work out with him. We all huddled in our bags, laughing. The way he channeled that energy, he had so much more than most people."

Lowe never pressured any of his children to pursue climbing. But he also believed that they could learn important lessons about life by observing his own approach to mountaineering. "I hope that [my sons] see in me the ability to believe in yourself and follow your passion — be passionate about something. That's my fundamental desire for them."

Final Triumphs—And Tragedy

In the summer of 1999 Lowe and two other climbers—Synnott and Jared Ogden—made the first successful ascent of the northwest face of Great Trango Tower, a 20,618-foot peak in the Karakoram Range of Northern Pakistan. This expedition was an incredibly difficult one, for the Tower is possibly the biggest sheer wall of rock on earth. During the last two weeks of the ascent, Lowe and his two climbing partners slept in little tents suspended from the side of the great wall, lashed by wind and snow. Each night, all that separated their bodies from the field of ice and rocks that lay thousands of feet below were their sleeping bags, their sleeping mats, and the thin fabric of their tents. But Lowe and his partners persevered, and they eventually bagged one of mountaineering's greatest unclaimed prizes.

Still, friends say that a summer 1999 trip to the top of Wyoming's Grand Teton mountain was Lowe's favorite climb of that year. He had stood atop the mountain more than 100 times in his life. His 1999 ascent, however, marked the first time that he had ever climbed a peak with his oldest son, Max. Lowe never pressured any of his children to pursue climbing. But he also believed that they could learn important lessons about life by observing his own approach to mountaineering. "I hope that [my sons] see in me the ability to believe in yourself and follow your passion—be passionate about something," he said. "That's my fundamental desire for them."

*Lowe, right, poses atop the 13,700-foot-high Grand Teton in Grand Teton
National Park in Wyoming with his son Max, left, fellow climber Tom Bozeman
and his son Jared, after their ascent in early September, 1999.*

A few weeks after his father-son expedition to the top of Grand Teton,
Lowe traveled to Tibet, deep in the Himalayan mountains. He was part of
an expedition that intended to climb a 26,291-foot peak called Shisha-
pangma, the world's 13th-highest mountain. The party then planned to
ski all the way back down, a feat that would give them a record for the
longest ski descent in history.

In early October, Lowe and the other members of the climbing party established a camp at the base of the mountain. "It is wonderful to be
back," said Lowe in an electronic "diary" that appeared all around the
world on the Internet. "Back among mountains that remind us of our vul-
nerability, our ultimate lack of control over the world we live in.
Mountains that demand humility, and yield so much peace in return."

83

On October 5, the expedition members woke up to a clear and beautiful day. Lowe and three other climbers decided to investigate an area of mountain slope that they planned to ski down after reaching the summit. As they reached the area, however, a huge section of snow and ice located more than a mile above them came loose from the mountain. The snow and ice quickly created a massive avalanche that rumbled down the slope toward the climbers. Two of the mountaineers barely escaped the fluke avalanche. But Lowe and Dave Bridges, an experienced mountain guide, photographer, and former paragliding champion, were killed in the slide. Their bodies were never recovered, and probably never will be.

―――― " ――――

Fellow climber Todd Skinner said, "Alex was pure Montana in an age of Hollywood. He showed us that you can be great—even the best in the world—and not lose character or genuine passion. It takes a lot to keep the flame burning so hot. Alex kept his own burning, and at the same time, he was the one who started the fire in a lot of others."

―――― " ――――

Lowe's Legacy

News of Lowe's death stunned climbers all around the world. Many people found it especially hard to accept that Lowe—who had always been known for his technical skill and good climbing judgment—had been lost in a freak avalanche. But mountaineers all over the world agreed that he had left a substantial legacy for future climbers. Lowe "represented something of the American spirit that we all hunger for," said Wiltsie. "He inspired so many people." Fellow climber Todd Skinner offered similar sentiments. "Alex was pure Montana in an age of Hollywood. He showed us that you can be great—even the best in the world—and not lose character or genuine passion. It takes a lot to keep the flame burning so hot. Alex kept his own burning, and at the same time, he was the one who started the fire in a lot of others."

MARRIAGE AND FAMILY

Lowe met his future wife, Jennifer Leigh, in 1980, and they married in 1983. They had three children together—Max, Sam, and Isaac. Jennifer is now a successful artist. "I don't regret a day spent with Alex," she said several weeks after his death. "I think my life with him was completely worth it. I would do it again if I had that choice, even knowing the outcome."

WRITINGS

Ice Climbing with Alex Lowe, 1997 (with Steven Boga)

FURTHER READING

Periodicals

Arizona Republic, Nov. 2, 1995, p.C1
Climbing, Aug. 1996, p.44; Feb. 1997, p.68; May 1998, p.24; Nov. 1999,
    p.20; Feb. 2000, p.58
Guardian (London), Oct. 8, 1999, p.12
Independent (London), Oct. 8, 1999, p.6
Los Angeles Times, Aug. 13, 1999, p.D8; Oct. 6, 1999, p.A3
National Geographic, Feb. 1998, p.46; Jan. 1999, p.70
National Geographic Adventure, Winter 1999, p.22
New York Times, Oct. 7, 1999, p.C23
People, Oct. 25, 1999, p.155
Outside, Mar. 1999; Dec. 1999, p.24; Dec. 1999, p.28
Skiing, Jan. 2000, p.40
Sports Afield, Feb. 2000, p.80
Sports Illustrated, Oct. 18, 1999, p.29
Time, Oct. 18, 1999, p.41

WORLD WIDE WEB SITE

http://www.mountainzone.com/climbing/99/interviews/lowe

Randy Moss 1977-

American Professional Football Player with the
Minnesota Vikings
1998 NFL Rookie of the Year

BIRTH

Randy Moss was born on February 13, 1977, in Rand, West
Virginia. He was raised by his mother, Maxine Moss, who
worked as a nurse's aide to provide for him and her two
other children, Latisia and Eric. Randy knew his father,
Randy Pratt, but had little contact with him during childhood.

YOUTH

Moss grew up in Rand, a small community outside of Charleston, West Virginia. As a youngster, he spent nearly all of his free time playing sports in the backyards, playgrounds, and streets of his neighborhood. "We played football and basketball anywhere we could find a game," he recalled. "That was the only thing happening." The only time that Moss and his buddies took a break from sports was at the height of summer, when they spent their afternoons diving and splashing around at the local swimming hole.

Moss saw his father from time to time, but his mother was the one who looked after him. "My mom raised me, and I had to look beyond not having a father growing up," he said. "My mom kept us in school. I might have missed three days of class from the first to the sixth grade. I was always pushed to go to school every day. In junior high school and high school, sick or not, I was always out the door." Years later, Moss credited his mother with protecting and guiding him during his youth. "My mom is my hero," he said simply.

EDUCATION

An All-Around Athlete

After completing elementary school in Rand, Moss enrolled at DuPont High School in nearby Belle, West Virginia. During his years at DuPont, he emerged as one of the finest all-around athletes in the school's history. As a sophomore, he won both the 100- and 200-meter track events at the state championships, and he excelled at baseball as well. But his best sports were basketball and football, where he used his height (6 feet, 4 inches), speed, and lean frame to great advantage.

On the basketball court, Moss teamed with future NBA star Jason Williams to lead one of the most potent basketball squads in all of West Virginia. A dominating scorer and rebounder, Moss was recognized as the state's top high school basketball player at the end of both his junior and senior seasons. He also bested a field of the country's top high school players to win a national slam dunk competition during his senior year. But amazingly enough, many observers believed that Moss's best sport was football.

Moss first emerged as one of West Virginia's top football players during his junior year, when he became the state's top two-way threat. On offense, he sailed through opposing secondaries to snare 40 passes and make 14 touchdowns. On defense he tallied 63 tackles, 7 interceptions, and a 35.5 yards-per-kick punting average. His excellent play on both sides of the ball caught the attention of major college programs around the country, including such powerhouse schools as Florida State and Notre Dame.

——  ——

Moss saw his father from time to time, but his mother was the one who looked after him. "My mom raised me, and I had to look beyond not having a father growing up," he said. "My mom kept us in school. I might have missed three days of class from the first to the sixth grade. I was always pushed to go to school every day. In junior high school and high school, sick or not, I was always out the door." Years later, Moss credited his mother with protecting and guiding him during his youth. "My mom is my hero," he said simply.

—— 〃 ——

Moss posted an even more impressive senior season on the gridiron, winning state Player of the Year honors. He caught 39 passes, scored 16 touchdowns, and became known as a threat to score any time he touched the ball. Opposing coaches focused their entire game plans on stopping the young star, only to watch him lead the DuPont offense up and down the field. "Randy Moss was the best high school football player I've ever seen," recalled Notre Dame Head Coach Lou Holtz. "He was unbelievable."

Impressed by Moss's unique blend of size, speed, and athleticism, Notre Dame offered the young star a scholarship. He quickly accepted, for Notre Dame had been his favorite team ever since his early childhood. But only a few months before his high school graduation, an ugly episode of violence ended Moss's dreams of playing for the Fighting Irish.

A Violent Confrontation

During Moss's years at DuPont High School, racial tensions between the mostly white student body and the school's black minority were a constant problem. In March 1995, these tensions exploded into violence. One day, a white student at DuPont carved a racial slur into a desk and showed it to one of Moss's black friends. The two boys got into a fight in front of Moss and several other students. As the fight progressed, the white student was knocked to the ground. At that point, Moss aimed two hard kicks at the fallen boy's body.

By the time the fight ended, the white student had suffered serious injuries, including a torn spleen and a concussion. As a participant in the beating, Moss was arrested and charged with felony assault. Moss apologized to the injured student for kicking him, and the charges were eventually reduced to misdemeanor battery. But Moss still received a sentence of 30 days in jail—which he was able to serve over a period of 18 months—and one year of probation. In addition, he was expelled from DuPont and forced to finish his high school education at Cabell Alternative School in West Virginia.

The ugly incident convinced the Notre Dame football program to withdraw its scholarship offer to Moss. This decision greatly disappointed Moss, who had badly wanted to play for the Irish. But a short time later, Florida State University (FSU) stepped in and offered Moss a full scholarship to play for their football team. The FSU coaching staff told him, however, that they would not let him play in any games during his freshman season. They wanted him to concentrate on adjusting to college life during his freshman year. Moss reluctantly agreed to the arrangement, which still allowed him to practice with the team. He graduated from Cabell Alternative School in West Virginia in 1995.

Moss attended FSU for one year. At the end of his freshman year, he reported to the authorities to complete his 30-day jail sentence (he only fulfilled part of the sentence before enrolling at FSU). But when he reported to legal authorities, a random drug test revealed that he had marijuana in his system. Moss's use of illegal drugs violated the terms of his probation and deepened his legal troubles. His probation was revoked and he was sentenced to an additional six months in jail. Florida State, meanwhile, decided to kick him off the team and take away his scholarship over this latest offense.

Moss spent the next several weeks in a West Virginia jail cell. During this time, he participated in a work-study program that allowed him to take day classes at West Virginia State, but he still had to spend nights and weekends behind bars. Moss later called this humiliating period the "low point" of his life. After serving 90 days of his six-month sentence, a judge granted him early release on July 26, 1996.

CAREER HIGHLIGHTS

College—Marshall University Thundering Herd

In the fall of 1996 Moss enrolled at Marshall University in Huntington, West Virginia. Marshall's football program was not as powerful as those at big universities. In fact, Marshall's program was classified as 1-AA, a notch below the 1-A classification that FSU, Notre Dame, and other big-time programs enjoyed. But Moss knew that student-athletes who transferred to 1-AA schools were permitted to play immediately, whereas transfers to 1-A programs were required to sit out for a year before playing.

When Moss arrived at Marshall, he vowed to clean up his act and concentrate on football. "I'm disappointed in myself for messing up chances at Notre Dame and Florida State," he said. "I'm trying to put that behind me and do what's best for Marshall." But legal problems continued to follow the talented young athlete. In November 1996 he got into an angry argument with Elizabeth Offutt, an ex-girlfriend who was the mother of his two-year-old daughter, Sydney. The two became involved in a shouting and shoving match that ended only after police arrived at the scene. At first, both Moss and Offutt were charged with domestic battery (unlawful beating of another person). The charges were eventually dismissed, but the incident did nothing to relieve widespread doubts about Moss's maturity and character.

Whatever his problems off the field, however, Moss quickly showed Marshall fans that he was still an awesome football player. He caught 78 passes over the course of the 1996 season, piling up 1,709 yards. He also set an NCAA single-season record of 28 touchdown catches and led all Division 1-AA players in kickoff returns. Moss's performance lifted the Marshall University Thundering Herd to an unbeaten 15-0 record and the school's first ever Division I-AA championship, a 49-29 victory over Montana. "He's as talented a player as I've ever been around," said Marshall Head Coach Bob Pruett. "He's electrifying."

Moss also showed that he was a "big game" player over the course of the season. In the 1996 championship game, for example, he romped through the Montana defense, catching nine passes for 220 yards and four touchdowns. "Moss is an incredible player," said one Montana defensive player after the game. "He single-handedly turned the tide of the game."

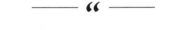

Moss's great 1996 season made him one of the nation's best-known college players. As the 1997 season approached, many football analysts speculated that he was a legitimate candidate for the Heisman Trophy, an annual award given to the nation's top college football player. But Moss tried not to get caught up in such these discussions. Instead, he talked about putting his legal troubles behind him and having another good season. "I don't blame anybody but myself for what's happened to me,"

"I don't blame anybody but myself for what's happened to me. I made some mistakes and I've paid the price. I feel blessed that I was able to land at Marshall and turn my life around. I'm confident that I'm headed in the right direction."

he said. "I made some mistakes and I've paid the price. I feel blessed that I was able to land at Marshall and turn my life around. I'm confident that I'm headed in the right direction."

More Controversy

But as the 1997 season unfolded, Moss continued to generate negative publicity for himself. He publicly expressed his dislike for the state of West Virginia, stating that he had been the victim of racism and unfair criticism about his legal troubles. He also got himself in hot water for his remarks about a 1970 plane crash that had killed the Marshall University football team and many school and community leaders. When asked by a reporter about the plane crash, Moss said that it "wasn't nothing big." The player's

Moss, right, pulls in a 6-yard touchdown pass from quarterback Jeff George dur-
ing a game between the Vikings and the Dallas Cowboys, November 8, 1999.

response triggered a tremendous uproar from people in Huntington and around the state. Moss quickly apologized for appearing insensitive. He explained that he meant to say that the crash happened before he was born, so that he did not know much about the tragedy. But the incident added to the cloud of controversy surrounding the young star.

In 1997 Marshall moved up to Division 1-A competition, joining the Mid-American Conference (MAC). As the season got underway, Moss quickly showed that he could still dominate a game. In one contest against Ball State, he tied a conference record by scoring 32 points in one game.

"Nobody in America is able to cover Moss," Ball State Coach Bill Lynch said afterward.

By the time the season ended, Moss had caught a conference-record 90 passes for 1,647 yards and 25 touchdowns, a new NCAA single-season record. He also won the Belitnikoff Award as the best college receiver in country, and finished fourth in the Heisman Trophy voting. Moss's spectacular sophomore season made him one of the best-known college football players in the entire country. But the young star expressed mixed feelings about his increasing fame. "It worries me how things are going to be [in the future]," he admitted. "If I were a normal person, I could go to the store and get me something to drink, drive to work, come home, watch a little TV and go to bed and wait for the next morning. But I can't go back on it. I've got to take what goes with all the stardom. I would just like to be normal."

At the end of the 1997 season, Moss decided to give up his last two years of eligibility and make himself available for the NFL draft. His decision sparked a tremendous amount of speculation about when he would be selected. All of the pro scouts agreed that he was the top wide receiver prospect in the entire draft. But many observers predicted that Moss's troubled past might convince some teams to pass him over in favor of a player who was not viewed as such a risky prospect.

In the May 1998 NFL draft, it quickly became evident that many teams harbored concerns about Moss's maturity and character. Team after team ignored him, choosing other players instead. He remained available until deep in the first round, when the Minnesota Vikings finally selected him as the 21st pick of the draft. Moss was happy to be selected by the Vikings. Minnesota had a talented team, and Randy's half-brother, Eric Moss, was a lineman on the team. But he could not help feeling a little bitter that so many teams had passed him over. "In athletic ability, I was probably in the top three [of college players available]," Moss later said. "In character, teams graded me down. They made the decision based on things that happened two or three years ago. At the end of the season, we'll see what rookie did the best."

The Minnesota Vikings

Moss signed a four-year, $4.5-million contract with Minnesota shortly after being drafted. Upon signing the contract, he stated that he planned to use some of his salary to take care of his mother and make her comfortable. "As much hard work as she put into raising the three of us, I'll see what she wants in life," he said. "Before I get a house, a car, before anything, . . . I'll see what she wants in life and makes sure it's done." He then turned his attention to preparing for the upcoming 1998 NFL season.

As Moss began his pre-season training, several veteran Vikings players made a special effort to help him deal with the ongoing press scrutiny. The player who helped Moss the most was star wide receiver Cris Carter. During his early years in the NFL, Carter had nearly ruined his career with drug abuse and other irresponsible behavior. But he had eventually matured into one of the league's best and most respected players. Armed with his own experiences, Carter believed that he could help Moss navigate through the traps that had nearly destroyed his own career.

During the summer of 1998, Carter spent a lot of time with Moss, talking with him about the benefits and drawbacks of athletic fame. "It was a friendship right away, because he trusted me," Carter said. "Randy knows I don't want anything from him, so he didn't have his guard up. . . . I tell him there are no excuses. He has been given a tremendous opportunity to mature and handle his life. He is young, but he shouldn't be any different than any other young players that they have brought in here before. They were all immature. You have to experience things to grow up, and he will." Carter also convinced Moss to take part in a grueling off-season workout program. "He never complained," Carter recalled. "There was not one thing I asked him to do that he did not do. There were times that he was sick, he was throwing up, he was hurting. He wanted to stop, but he never complained."

Rookie of the Year

When the 1998 season got underway, Moss immediately took the league by storm. Acting on his pre-season threat to "do whatever I can to rip this league up," he emerged as one of the NFL's top receivers. By midseason, many reporters were writing that the lanky receiver was the "steal of the draft." Vikings Head Coach Dennis Green praised his young star as well. "He is truly a great competitor," he said. "That is what I like the best about him. He loves to compete, loves to win. He has very high expectations for himself. And he is one of the most fun guys and really one of the most popular guys on our football team."

Moss's dangerous pass-catching ability helped transform the Viking offense into the league's top scoring machine. By the time the regular season came to a close, Minnesota had tallied a great 15-1 record and set a new NFL single-season scoring record with 556 points, almost 35 points a game. Moss, meanwhile, caught 69 passes for 1,313 yards. He also led

Evan Fridley receives an autograph from Moss, July 3, 1999.

the NFL in touchdown receptions with 17, a new rookie record. His performance earned him Rookie-of-the-Year honors and a spot on the NFL All-Pro Team. Moss's spectacular rookie season made him a fan favorite, and his number 84 purple jersey became the best-selling shirt in the entire country.

Minnesota's record-shattering offensive performance during the 1998 campaign convinced many people that the Vikings would cap their season with a trip to the Super Bowl. But the team lost to the Atlanta Falcons in an overtime thriller in the National Football Conference title game, 31-28.

A Repeat Performance

As the 1999 season approached, Moss predicted that he would have another big season. "How you going to stop Moss? How you going to do this? You can't stop Moss," he boasted. "They're still waiting on me to fall. I think they're ready to kiss my butt, but at the same time they're still ready for me to fall. I don't care because I've never been a person who really cared what other people think. I'm gonna go out there and play, 'cause I know that's money day, so I'm going out there to make money."

In the early stages of the 1999 season, however, Moss and the Vikings struggled. Hindered by a sputtering offense, the team managed only two victories in their first six games. After game six, however, Minnesota promoted Jeff George to the starting quarterback position. The switch worked, and before long the Viking offensive machine was rolling again. By the time the regular season ended, the Vikings had reached the playoffs. But Minnesota's season ended on a sour note, as they suffered a lopsided playoff defeat at the hands of the eventual Super Bowl champion St. Louis Rams.

Moss had another fine season in 1999. He caught 80 passes for 1,413 yards and 11 touchdowns during the campaign. In addition, he and Carter solidified their reputation as the top receiving duo in the entire National Football League over the course of the season. Nonetheless, Moss's reputation for rude or immature behavior continued to overshadow his accomplishments on the field to some degree. For example, during Minnesota's playoff loss to St. Louis, Moss squirted an official in the back with a water bottle after the official refused to call an opposing player for a pass interference penalty. Moss was fined $40,000 for this childish action.

Despite such incidents, however, many fans think that Minnesota's decision to draft Moss was a great one. In fact, many people believe that if Moss can stay healthy, he has a chance to develop into one of the leading receivers in NFL history. For his part, Moss believes that he has a long and productive career ahead of him. But he states that his career will be incomplete if he does not win a Super Bowl ring somewhere along the way.

HOME AND FAMILY

Randy Moss lives in the Minneapolis area. He is the father of two children, Sydney and Thaddeus, with Elizabeth Offutt.

HOBBIES AND OTHER INTERESTS

Moss spends a lot of his free time playing or watching basketball. In fact, some people have speculated that he might someday try to earn a spot on the roster of the Minnesota Timberwolves or some other NBA team. In addition, Moss enjoys playing the drums and listening to music.

HONORS AND AWARDS

Mr. Basketball (West Virginia high school player of the year): 1994, 1995
West Virginia State Player of the Year (football): 1995
Mid-American Conference (MAC) Player of the Year: 1997

Fred Belitnikoff Award (NCAA award to country's best college receiver): 1997
NFL All-Pro Team: 1998
NFL Rookie of the Year: 1998
Rookie of the Year Award (*Sporting News*): 1998
NFL Pro Bowl: 1998, 1999

FURTHER READING

Books

Who's Who in America, 2000

Periodicals

Detroit Free Press, Dec. 24, 1997, p.C1
Minneapolis Star Tribune, July 26, 1998, p.C1
New York Times, Dec. 23, 1999, p.C21; Feb. 7, 2000, p.D2
San Francisco Chronicle, Apr. 11, 1998, p.E1
Sport, Oct. 1997, p.58; Aug. 1999, p.50; Mar. 2000, p.30
Sporting News, Sep. 16, 1996, p.44; Nov. 16, 1998, p.14; Jan. 25, 1999, p.12
Sports Illustrated, Aug. 25, 1997, p.130; Jan. 18, 1999, p.54
Sports Illustrated for Kids, Feb. 1999, p.50; Jan. 2000, p.32
St. Louis Post Dispatch, Jan. 16, 2000, p.D7
USA Today, Dec. 19, 1996; Dec. 23, 1996; Jan. 9, 1998; Aug. 24, 1999

ADDRESS

Minnesota Vikings
9529 Viking Drive
Eden Prairie, MN 55344

WORLD WIDE WEB SITE

http://www.nfl.com

Se Ri Pak 1977-

South Korean Golfer
Winner of the U.S. Women's Open and the LPGA
Championship in 1998

BIRTH

Se Ri Pak (pronounced suh-REE pock) was born on September 28, 1977, in the city of Daejeon, a suburb of Seoul, the capital of South Korea. Her father, Joon Chul Pak, and mother, Jeong Sook Kim, own a construction business. Se Ri has an older sister, Yoo Ri, and a younger sister, Ae Ri.

YOUTH

Starting to Play Golf

Se Ri Pak was introduced to golf at the age of 11 by her father, who had been an amateur golf champion in South Korea in the 1980s. Joon Chul Pak could see that his daughter had a talent for golf, but he decided it would be best to let her choose whether to pursue the sport. For a while, Se Ri participated in track and field instead. She excelled at sprinting, the hurdles, and the shot put, among other events. When she was 14, however, her father took her to a local junior golf tournament, hoping that it would spark her interest in the sport. "I saw all the green grass, the fresh air, the people dressed well," she recalled. "I decided I wanted to change."

By the time Se Ri committed herself to the game, she and her father knew that her skills were far behind those of other golfers her age. In order to make up for lost time, they embarked on a rigorous schedule of training and practice. Joon Chul would wake his daughter up at 5:30 in the morning. The first thing she would do was run up and down the steps of their apartment building—15 stories in all. This activity would be followed by six or more hours of practice each day. "My wife worried that I would kill Se Ri," Joon Chul admitted. "And for what, a game that was not so popular in Korea? But I was very straight, very stern with Se Ri about her golf because I believed she had the talent, the patience to one day be a great player in the world."

A Demanding Coach

Joon Chul was determined to make his daughter's mental conditioning as tough as her physical training. If Se Ri failed to make a shot, he would hit her with a stick called a *pechori.* To make Se Ri fearless on the golf course, her father made her confront one of her fears—cemeteries. First, she practiced golf near a cemetery. Then she and her father camped out overnight in one. Finally, Se Ri had to spend the night alone in a tent in a cemetery. Se Ri has acknowledged the difficulty of her father's approach to coaching. "He wanted me to win everything—not second, not third, but win," she noted. "But people are not machines. Sometimes I miss an easy one, and he was angry, he keeps pushing, 'What are you thinking? Why did you miss?' I was really upset, and I don't have anyone to talk to, so I would cry by myself in my room."

When Se Ri Pak became a well-known golfer, these stories shocked many people. They considered Joon Chul's training methods a form of child abuse. But Se Ri claims that she understands why her father did it. "He wanted to make me more strong, my body and my mind, everything, because the players [in the United States] are really strong. If I have to play, then I have to be strong," she stated. "I know he's sad before because I was only 15, 16, 17. I like to have fun with friends. But no friends, just practice. He knows I'm a little tired. But he knows what it's like here so he just kept pushing, he made me strong. So, I'm really happy [with] my Dad."

Joon Chul also had to make sacrifices in order to nurture his daughter's talent. There is only one public golf course in South Korea. As a result, golf is a sport that is usually played by only the wealthiest members of society. Once Se Ri showed her ability as a golfer, her father used nearly all of the family's savings to buy her a one-year membership at a golf course. When the membership ended, Se Ri was forced to do most of her practicing on the course during amateur tournaments. As her father invested more time and money in Se Ri's career, the family business began having financial problems. Her mother even took on a second job as a cook to earn additional money. Se Ri grew determined to succeed in order to repay her family for their sacrifices. "They were supporting me so I could play golf even though their business was failing," she recalled. "I started practicing very hard, not really knowing why. I kept saying to myself, 'Just wait and see, they're going to get everything they deserve, if I can help it.'"

> ――― " ―――
>
> *Se Ri has acknowledged the difficulty of her father's approach to coaching. "He wanted me to win everything—not second, not third, but win. But people are not machines. Sometimes I miss an easy one, and he was angry, he keeps pushing, 'What are you thinking? Why did you miss?' I was really upset, and I don't have anyone to talk to, so I would cry by myself in my room."*
>
> ――― " ―――

Se Ri's intense training quickly paid off with success in amateur tournaments in South Korea. At the age of 14—after having only played a few rounds on an actual golf course—she won the first junior tournament that she entered, the Lyle and Scott Tournament in Seoul.

EDUCATION

Shortly after her first success on the golf course, Pak enrolled at the Kumsung Women's High School, which had the top golf team in the na-

tion. Pak was a good student, but her schoolwork and social life took a distant second place to golf. In 1991, Pak won the student division of the Korea Herald Cup. The following year, she won the Presidential Cup Middle and High School League and finished tenth in the Korea Women's Open. Her success in golf convinced her to quit school and concentrate on becoming a professional golfer.

CAREER HIGHLIGHTS

Within a short time, Pak proved that she could compete with the best amateur golfers in the world. At 17, she won the Korean Junior Competition and played as a member of the Korean team at the 1994 World Amateur Team Championship in Paris. In 1995, she reached the semifinals of the U.S. Amateur Championship, where she lost her match to amateur golf star Kelli Kuehne. As an amateur, Pak won over 30 tournaments in a four-year time period.

Turns Professional in 1996

In 1996, at the age of 17, Pak became the youngest player ever to be admitted into the Korean Ladies Professional Golf Association, and that year she won the KLPGA Most Valuable Player Award for both professional and amateur performance. Pak signed a 10-year, $3.6 million endorsement deal with Samsung, one of South Korea's largest companies, which produces television and other electronic products. The contract was one of the largest ever awarded in women's golf. During her first year as a professional golfer, Pak proved that her sponsors were right in their assessment of her talent. She won six out of 14 KLPGA tournaments that she entered, and she also finished as runner-up seven times. In recognition of her success, she was declared a national hero by South Korea's president, Kim Dae Jung.

Pak moved to the United States at the beginning of 1997. To look after its investment, Samsung hired Sung Yong (Steven) Kil, a former sportswriter, to be her business manager. He also served as her secretary, press agent, and interpreter. In the meantime, Pak began training with one of the best golf instructors in the world, David Leadbetter, who had coached such male professional golfers as Nick Faldo and Greg Norman. Leadbetter was not known for coaching female players, and he initially expressed reservations about working with Pak. But he changed his mind once he saw her swing. "You could always tell somebody has great ability in golf to strike the ball well because it is just a different sound about the strike. The sound that she had on the shot was very similar to the male tour players. This was very impressive," he recalled. "You only so often get young players who come along who just have so much talent."

In June 1997, Pak made her U.S. professional debut at the Michelob Light Classic in St. Louis, Missouri. She went on to play—and to play well enough to win prize money—in the three most prestigious events in women's golf: the U.S. Women's Open, the du Maurier Classic, and the Women's British Open. Before she had even turned 20, Pak had won over $750,000. Returning to a warm welcome in South Korea, Pak won the Korean Rose Open and the Seoul Ladies Open.

Perhaps the highlight of Pak's first pro season in the United States was participating in the highly competitive LPGA Qualifying Tournament. This event determines which golfers will receive one of three dozen Tour Cards. Tour Cards enable new golfers to enter LPGA tournaments during the following year. Pak performed well on the first day of the tournament. On the second day she posted a disappointing score. On the third day, however, she rebounded to shoot one of her best rounds ever.

During that round, Pak amazed fellow competitors and spectators by hitting six birdies in a row. In golf, the difficulty of each hole is determined by the number of shots allowed for its completion, known as "par." For example, a hole that requires four strokes to complete is a "par 4." If the player makes the hole in one shot fewer than par, the score is called a "birdie." If the player makes the hole in one shot greater than par, the score is called a "bogey." A typical round of golf—always 18 holes—usually involves a total par of around 72 strokes. Golfers compete to achieve the lowest total score at the end of several rounds. Pak's score for the final round of the tournament was 10 under par. She thus set a new tournament record for a round and tied for first place overall in the tournament.

The 1998 LPGA Championship

By winning the 1997 LPGA Qualifying Tournament, Pak earned a place on the prestigious LPGA Tour for the 1998 season. This meant that she would compete against the best female golfers in the world. Pak started out slowly, with a top finish of eleventh in the year's first few events. But she emerged as a top contender in her first major tournament, the LPGA Championship.

Wet weather on the first day of the tournament worked to Pak's advantage. The damp grass tended to prevent the players' shots from rolling very far on the ground. For this reason, most of the players had to aim for no better than par on the long, par-five holes. But Pak's powerful swing enabled her to hit the ball long enough and high enough to make several birdies. She ended the first day with a one-stroke lead. On the second day, she extended her lead to two strokes.

> *Pak grew determined to succeed in order to repay her family for their sacrifices. "They were supporting me so I could play golf even though their business was failing. I started practicing very hard, not really knowing why. I kept saying to myself, 'Just wait and see, they're going to get everything they deserve, if I can help it.'"*

On the third day of the tournament, Pak showed her mental toughness. On one difficult hole, she hit the ball from the tee into the water. After placing a new ball on the grass and taking a penalty stroke, she hit a shot of almost 200 yards and ended up making par on the hole. Even though she lost her first place position for the day because of a bogey on the 17th

hole, she came back on the final day of the tournament and won the event. Pak thus became the youngest winner of a major LPGA tournament in 30 years.

Pak's next triumph was the 1998 U.S. Women's Open, where terrible weather transformed the difficult course into a daunting challenge. By the end of the second day, Pak had overcome rain, lightning, and high winds to gain the lead. She held onto this position during the third round. By the end of the fourth day, however, an American amateur named Jenny Chuasiriporn had tied Pak for first place. As a result, the two leaders were required to face each other the next day for an 18-hole playoff round.

During the playoff, Chuasiriporn had an opportunity to win the tournament. But—apparently because of nerves—she failed to make the winning putt. For the first time in the history of the U.S. Women's Open, the winner would be decided by "sudden death." The two leaders would continue playing additional holes until one of them scored better than the other. Despite the nerve-wracking tension, Pak managed to make a birdie on the second hole of the sudden-death round. She won the 1998 U.S. Women's Open, becoming the youngest woman ever to win two major golf tournaments in one year.

Pak followed her U.S. Women's Open victory with two more wins in the same month. At the Jamie Farr Classic, she won the tournament with a four-day total score of 261, the lowest total score ever posted in an LPGA tournament. Pak then won the Giant Eagle LPGA Classic, which gave her the most tournament wins by an LPGA rookie in 20 years. "I really surprise[d] myself," she said of her successful rookie season. "I knew I could win tournaments in this country, but not that fast. I thought I [would] win tournaments two years, three years later. By that time, I know many things, about the golf courses, about this country. But this is [my] first year. I don't know that much. Everything's new."

"I really surprise[d] myself," she said of her successful rookie season. "I knew I could win tournaments in this country, but not that fast. I thought I [would] win tournaments two years, three years later. By that time, I know many things, about the golf courses, about this country. But this is [my] first year. I don't know that much. Everything's new."

Career Changes

Pak received a great deal of attention for her outstanding rookie season on the LPGA Tour. She became a hero to many people in South Korea, and she was invited to the White House as a guest of the South Korean president, who was visiting Washington, D.C. But all the publicity also had a down side. Pak became increasingly tired as she attempted to fulfill

Si Ri Pak holds up the trophy filled with cash after winning the LPGA tour championship at the Desert Inn Golf Club in Las Vegas, 1998.

the expectations of her sponsor, Samsung, that she play in as many tournaments as possible. She was finally hospitalized for exhaustion and a severe cold while visiting her homeland in the fall of 1998. But she was so popular with the South Korean people that a reporter invaded her privacy and photographed her in her hospital bed.

At this point, Pak decided that she needed to make some changes in her life. "I learned that I'd have to do a better job looking after me," she explained. "Nobody else could do it. I had to." Pak followed through on this decision by making dramatic changes to her career. She renegotiated her contract with Samsung. Then she fired the business manager they had appointed for her, Steven Kil, and signed with International Management Group, which also manages golf superstar Tiger Woods. She also fired her coach, David Leadbetter, because she felt that he was not devoting enough time to her.

The stress of her illness and her quick rise to fame took a toll on Pak at the beginning of the 1999 season. Her second year on the LPGA tour began slowly. But Pak broke through for a victory in June at the ShopRite LPGA Classic. She followed this success by winning a tense playoff against five other golfers at the Jamie Farr Kroger Classic. In September 1999, Pak came from behind to win the Samsung World Championship of Women's Golf by one stroke.

"I see other 21-year-olds, and I realize I've given up some things. I've had to work hard, but it has been worth it. I love golf. This is the life I want. I don't want to have just one good year. I want a great career. Sometimes when you push hard, things get worse. But I feel my best is still ahead."

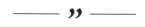

The highlight of Pak's 1999 season came in the final event of the year, the PageNet LPGA Tour Championship in November. After finishing the last round in a tie with Karrie Webb and Laura Davies, Pak faced a difficult shot on the first playoff hole. Her drive landed behind a tree, and she had to make a perfect approach shot to the green in order to avoid the obstacle. She did, and the ball landed three feet from the hole for an easy birdie putt. Pak thus won her fourth tournament of the season, tying her total from her great rookie year.

In 2000, Pak once again started the season slowly, posting only one top 10 finish in her first six tournaments. Despite the difficult times, however, Pak is determined to have a long and successful career as a professional golfer. "I see other 21-year-olds, and I realize I've given up some things," she explained. "I've had to work hard, but it has been worth it. I love golf. This is the life I want. I don't want to have just one good year. I want a great career. Sometimes when you push hard, things get worse. But I feel my best is still ahead."

HOME AND FAMILY

Pak, who is not married, lives in Orlando, Florida, in a home she shares with a miniature schnauzer named Happy. She remains close to her family in South Korea and speaks to them on the telephone every day. Despite the distance between them, Pak admits that she has struggled to develop a degree of independence from her parents. "I want to be stronger. I want to grow up, in my thinking, in my golf game, in my life. I have to make decisions myself, only me, with no help," she stated. "Korean culture is different. Just because you are 22, 23, or 25 years old doesn't mean you can say 'no' to mom and dad. It's not that easy for me."

In the United States, Pak has received help both professionally and personally from her idol, LPGA legend Nancy Lopez, who made her mark on women's golf more than 20 years ago. "Se Ri's got to find what makes her happy, because that's what is going to help her win, not trying to satisfy everybody else. She has the press . . . in her face all the time, and she has no time to breathe," Lopez noted. "Sometimes I just want to stand in front of everybody and say 'Hey, leave her alone.' I needed somebody to do that for me."

HOBBIES AND OTHER INTERESTS

When she is not practicing or competing, Pak studies the English language and enjoys playing video games. She frequently eats traditional Korean foods, such as soybean paste stew or pickled spice cabbage stew, at a Korean restaurant near her Florida home.

HONORS AND AWARDS

Korean Junior Competition: 1994
KLPGA Most Valuable Player: 1996, 1997
Associated Press Female Athlete of the Year: 1998
LPGA Rookie of the Year: 1998
U.S. Women's Open Championship: 1998
LPGA Championship: 1998

FURTHER READING

Books

Sports Stars, Series 5, 1999
Stewart, Mark. *Se Ri Pak: Driven to Win*, 2000 (juvenile)
Who's Who in America, 2000

Periodicals

Business Week, Aug. 17, 1998, p.68
Current Biography 1999
Newsweek, July 27, 1998, p.50
New York Times, July 28, 1998, p.C1; June 2, 1999, p.D8
New York Times Magazine, Oct. 18, 1998, p.82
People, Aug. 24, 1998, p.115
Seattle Post-Intelligencer, Sep. 10, 1998, p.C1
Sports Illustrated, July 13, 1998, p.44; Aug. 3, 1998, p.52
USA Today, Oct. 30, 1998, p.C24
Washington Post, Oct. 25, 1998, p.D20

ADDRESS

LPGA
100 International Golf Dr.
Daytona Beach, FL 32124

WORLD WIDE WEB SITES

http://www.lpga.com/tour/bios/Pak.html
http://www.golfonline.com

Dawn Riley 1964-

American Yacht Racer
Only Person to Compete in Two Whitbread Round-
the-World Races and Three America's Cup Series

BIRTH

Dawn Riley was born on July 21, 1964, in Detroit, Michigan.
She was the first of three children born to Chuck Riley, an
advertising executive, and Prudence Riley, a massage thera-
pist and homemaker. She has a younger sister, Dana, and a
younger brother, Todd.

YOUTH

Riley inherited a passion for sailing from her family. "My grandfather was a sailmaker on the Great Lakes, and we always owned a boat and raced," she explained. "I started sailing when I was a month old—after my baptism my whole family went out on the boat." Riley started steering her parents' 25-foot sailboat at the age of five, even though she could barely see over the top of the cabin. "She'd sing songs and was quite delighted," her father remembered.

When Riley was in eighth grade, her parents pulled the children out of school for a year and sailed to the Caribbean and back. They traveled through the Great Lakes, down the Hudson River, up the Atlantic Coast to Maine, then all the way down past Florida to the Bahamas and the Virgin Islands. The trip convinced young Dawn that she wanted to spend her life at sea. "We saw things we never would have seen had we stayed at home: endless horizons, dolphins who escorted us through the ocean, island waterfalls, coral reefs swarming with Technicolor fish, and people who did not live like the people at home in Detroit," Riley wrote in her book *Taking the Helm*.

Upon returning to Michigan, the Rileys bought a house on a canal off of Lake St. Clair, which is part of the Great Lakes system. Dawn joined a youth sailboat racing program on Lake St. Clair. "As soon as the snow thawed and the water got warm enough for sailing, I was rushing from school to go out on boats," she noted. She also hung around local yacht clubs and pestered sailboat owners until they let her join their crew for regattas (races). At first, some people doubted Riley's abilities because she was a girl. But as she got older and more experienced, the skippers began inviting her to participate in races all over the Great Lakes. She dreamed of someday becoming the captain of her own boat and racing in the prestigious America's

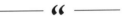

"My grandfather was a sailmaker on the Great Lakes, and we always owned a boat and raced. I started sailing when I was a month old—after my baptism my whole family went out on the boat." Riley started steering her parents' 25-foot sailboat at the age of five, even though she could barely see over the top of the cabin. "She'd sing songs and was quite delighted," her father remembered.

Cup. "Every since I was young, I wanted to do things first and best," she stated. "I always dreamed high."

EDUCATION

Riley attended South Lake High School in St. Clair Shores and L'Anse Cruise High School in Harrison Township, two communities north of Detroit and on Lake St. Clair. In addition to racing sailboats after school, she ran track and set a school record in the discus throw. She also became the first girl to play the tuba in the marching band. During Riley's senior year of high school, her parents got divorced. This situation put a strain on the family's finances, so she didn't have the money to go away to college. Instead, she attended nearby Macomb Community College for two years and worked at odd jobs to earn money. Then she went to Michigan State University for her junior and senior years of college. At MSU, Riley raced small, two-person boats as captain of the sailing team. She graduated with a bachelor's degree in advertising in 1986.

CAREER HIGHLIGHTS

After graduating from college, Riley initially planned to move to New York City and work in a big advertising agency. When she had trouble finding a "real" job, however, she naturally gravitated back toward the water. She taught sailing lessons, moved boats from one port to another for wealthy owners, and scrubbed the bottoms of boats. Whenever she could, she joined the crews of racing sailboats for regattas. "I wanted most of all to be racing," she stated. "But as a woman, it was always a case of proving I was strong enough, a good enough sailor, and able to fit into the mostly male society on board—whether it was as raunchy as a locker room or as polite as a tea party. It was always an uphill battle, but I was willing to put up a fight."

The 1989-90 Whitbread Round-the-World Race

By the late 1980s, Riley had built up an impressive resume of racing experience on the Great Lakes and on the ocean. In 1989, she heard that a British woman named Tracy Edwards was putting together an all-woman crew to compete in the Whitbread Round-the-World Race. This race, which is held every four years and covers 32,000 miles of ocean, is considered the toughest sailboat race in the world. Edwards had competed in the race once before, as a cook aboard a boat with 17 men. She wanted to compete as a sailor this time, and to give other women a chance to compete as well.

America True *co-ed crew.*

The Whitbread is divided into six sections, or legs. Racers begin their nine-month journey in Southampton, England, and sail southward through the Atlantic and across the Equator to Punta del Este, Uruguay, on the coast of South America. The second leg takes them eastward around the southern tip of Africa to Fremantle, Australia. From there they continue around the southern coast of Australia to Auckland, New Zealand. The fourth leg of the race, which is often the most treacherous, crosses the South Pacific Ocean around the southern tip of South America then returns to Uruguay. From there, competitors sail northward through the Atlantic and across the Equator to Ft. Lauderdale, Florida. Finally, the sixth leg takes them eastward across the Atlantic to the finish in Southampton.

Riley knew that competing in the Whitbread with the first all-woman crew in the history of the event was a great opportunity. She faxed her resume to Edwards, and the captain sent her a plane ticket to England in response. Edwards received 460 applications from women interested in joining her crew, and she interviewed 100 women. She selected Riley because of her varied racing experience and her extensive knowledge of boats. Riley thus joined a crew of 12 women from 11 countries on board the *Maiden,* a 58-foot racing sailboat.

Before the race started, the longest consecutive time Riley had ever spent at sea was a week. But some legs of the Whitbread would take a month. Altogether, she could look forward to spending most of a year living in cramped quarters with 11 other women. Because of space limitations, the crew members were allowed to bring very little clothing or personal items on board *Maiden*. While they were at sea, they ate freeze-dried food and could not take a shower. The crew was divided into two watches that worked on deck for alternating four-hour shifts. Then they returned to their cramped bunks below deck and tried to sleep. "You do get worn down," Riley admitted.

As they sailed around the world, the crew of the *Maiden* faced conditions ranging from searing tropical heat to extreme cold. They also encountered high winds, huge waves, dangerous icebergs, and terrible storms. In one particularly serious crisis, Riley found herself trying to fix an electrical problem in rough seas with three feet of water inside the cabin. Still, the women worked together to overcome the obstacles. They ended up winning two early legs of the race in their division (competing boats were placed in four divisions based on size and speed) before giving up the lead in light winds on leg 4.

> *Even though* **Maiden** *did not win the race, Riley felt that the crew had proved something just by completing the most grueling sailing race on earth. "In the beginning people were skeptical," she noted. "We went from people telling us we were crazy, that we were all going to die, and by the time we got back to England, we were heroes."*

The all-woman crew of the *Maiden* attracted a great deal of attention during the race. In New Zealand, for example, 10,000 people turned out to greet them at the docks when they arrived after midnight. Even though *Maiden* did not win the race, Riley felt that the crew had proved something just by completing the most grueling sailing race on earth. "In the beginning people were skeptical," she noted. "We went from people telling us we were crazy, that we were all going to die, and by the time we got back to England, we were heroes."

The 1992 America's Cup

After completing the Whitbread, Riley set her sights on competing for sailing's most prestigious trophy, the America's Cup. The first America's Cup race was held in 1851 between the United States and England. The schooner *America* won the race for the United States, so the trophy was named the America's Cup. It belonged to the New York Yacht Club for 132 years, as a series of American sailboats successfully defended it.

The race is held every three to four years, each time featuring top boats from around the world. The country that is the current champion of the America's Cup holds a series of races to select the best sailboat to defend it. In the meantime, boats from as many as a dozen other countries compete to earn the right to challenge the champion. Two boats — the defender and the top challenger — then meet in a best-of-nine series of races in the defender's home waters to decide who takes home the Cup. The America's Cup event attracts the best sailors from around the world. The teams representing the competing nations spend millions of dollars to build the most technologically advanced boats possible under the rules. In the head-to-head match races, victories sometimes come down to a matter of seconds.

In 1983, American skipper Dennis Conner lost the Cup to an Australian boat with a revolutionary new design. Conner reclaimed the Cup for the United States in 1987, and then he successfully defended it two years later against New Zealand. In 1992, Riley was selected to be a member of the crew for *America3* (pronounced "America cubed"), which was competing to defend the Cup for the United States. She was the only woman among the 38 sailors who crewed on the team's two 75-foot boats. In fact, she was the only woman on any crew competing for the Cup that year. A few women had sailed in the America's Cup in the past, but they had not played active roles on the crew. "In the 1800s, Cup boats had oriental rugs and fireplaces. When a woman sailed back then, her job was to make sure the ashes didn't get on the rugs," Riley explained. "[But] this is modern-day sailing. We're not sipping martinis under an umbrella out there."

Riley took a position in the pit for the *America3* team. The pit is considered the vital nerve center of a racing sailboat. Riley's job was to raise and lower sails as needed and coordinate what the people in the bow (front) and stern (rear) of the boat were doing. Her position required strength, endurance, good instincts, and a strong understanding of all the other positions on board. "She anticipates the maneuvers and has a great sense of timing," said the boat's skipper, Gary Jobson. Riley emphasized that she was not just a token female on the crew. "I am not here because I am a woman," she stated. "I'm no different from anyone else. I'm not trying to do something I can't do. I'm a competent ocean-racing crewman."

Riley remained with *America3* throughout the preparations for the America's Cup defender trials. Shortly before the official races began,

however, she was told that she would not be on the 16-member crew that would race the team's top boat against Dennis Conner for the right to defend the America's Cup. Riley was deeply disappointed that she could not be on the water. But she continued to support the team as

America3 won the trials and went on to defend the Cup successfully against New Zealand in the finals. Afterward, team organizer Bill Koch announced that he planned to organize a 16-member all-women's team to compete in the 1995 event.

The 1993-94 Whitbread Round-the-World Race

As the 1993-94 Whitbread approached, Riley originally hoped to gather her own co-ed crew to compete in the endurance event. Unable to secure funding, she eventually gave up on the idea of participating in the race. She knew that an American woman named Nance Frank had entered with an all-woman crew on board the *U.S. Women's Challenge*. But Riley was not particularly interested in joining another female crew for the event. "Been there, done that," she explained. Riley felt that the success of *Maiden* had already proved that women were capable of competing in the Whitbread. She only planned to enter the grueling around-the-world race a second time if she could put together her own team and have a chance to win.

As Riley sat at home, the *U.S. Women's Challenge* struggled through the first leg of the Whitbread. The boat was poorly equipped and had serious problems on the voyage to Uruguay, including a weathered mainsail that ripped six different times. In the meantime, the members of the crew experienced personality clashes and had terrible disagreements. When the boat finally reached Punta del Este, Uruguay, several crew members quit the team. They said that Frank's lack of experience and shortage of funding had made them fearful for their safety on the next leg of the race. In response, Frank officially withdrew the *U.S. Women's Challenge* from the Whitbread.

As it turned out, Frank did not own the boat, because she had fallen behind on her lease payments. The boat's owners, a Florida-based company

> "
>
> *"I want to prove* **Maiden** *wasn't a fluke, that problems involved before I came were because of other things, not because we're women.*
> *I want to have a really strong team by the end of this, and then, looking back a year later, I'll have learned things like team-building, crew politics, and management skills that you can't get anywhere but in the skipper's spot—and it's not always fun."*
>
> "

117

> ## "
>
> *"Some days the sun gleamed off the ice; the seals waved hello with their fins and the penguins swam by, and they welcomed us to a magical mystery tour of this place that is free from human beings, unbound by land, and endless. Some days, the ocean was a gray planet with no life at all: everything was still and frozen and desolate.*
>
> ## "

called Ocean Ventures, decided that they wanted the vessel to continue the race. They took legal steps to gain possession of it and then asked Riley to take over as captain. She reluctantly agreed and flew to Uruguay on a few days' notice. "I want to prove *Maiden* wasn't a fluke, that problems involved before I came were because of other things, not because we're women," she explained. "I want to have a really strong team by the end of this, and then, looking back a year later, I'll have learned things like team-building, crew politics, and management skills that you can't get anywhere but in the skipper's spot—and it's not always fun."

Riley immediately began making repairs on the boat and trying to gather a crew. Her final group of women included five new additions and seven former members of Frank's crew. They began the second leg of the race, which included a dangerous passage through the South Pacific Ocean, with very little preparation. "We had 15 minutes of practice before the start," Riley recalled. "The boat was held together with Popsicle sticks and duct tape." Unfortunately, they continued to experience equipment problems, and Leg 2 turned into a very difficult journey.

"Some days the sun gleamed off the ice; the seals waved hello with their fins and the penguins swam by, and they welcomed us to a magical mystery tour of this place that is free from human beings, unbound by land, and endless," Riley remembered in her account of the race, *Taking the Helm*. "Some days, the ocean was a gray planet with no life at all: everything was still and frozen and desolate. Some days, the ocean came alive to inspire terror: every time the boat pounded off a wave, it seemed as if the hull would explode; every time a gust of wind hit, you waited for the sails or the rigging to blow up in your face. With every mood, the feeling of anticipation—of what the next day or the next nightfall would bring—was almost the worst part."

By the time Riley and her crew staggered into Fremantle, Australia, they were a week behind the leader of their division. But when they arrived, they learned that the Dutch brewery Heineken had signed on to sponsor them. They suddenly had enough money to make all the needed repairs on the boat and purchase better equipment and supplies. The boat was renamed *Heineken* and received a shiny new paint job. "I'm really grateful to Heineken for making it possible to continue," Riley stated. "It's a huge psychological boost to have a boat that looks so great. It looks fast just tied up to the pier. That kind of thing really helps morale."

Over the next legs of the Whitbread, *Heineken* performed well and made up lost time. But on the final leg, just 850 miles short of England, the boat lost its rudder (the device that controls the direction and allows steering) in high seas and gale force winds. The women struggled to rig a replacement rudder and barely limped into Southampton. Despite the poor finish, Riley received a great deal of praise and international recognition for her handling of the difficult situation. "Taking over a rebellious crew is risky enough business at the best of times," wrote the *Independent*. "Doing so a few days before putting to sea, to cross some of the most treacherous waters in the world, is almost an act of faith. . . . Dawn Riley was the woman who took that decision, but she had the background to make it." In 1995, Riley published a memoir about her experiences as captain of the *Heineken* called *Taking the Helm*.

The 1995 America's Cup

In 1995, *America3* team organizer Bill Koch invited Riley to be the captain of the all-woman crew on board the *Mighty Mary* during the America's Cup defender trials. Riley was pleased to have the opportunity to lead the first all-female crew in the long history of the prestigious yacht race.

Many people doubted whether a team of women could be competitive in the America's Cup. Their primary concern was that some of the positions aboard a racing sailboat require great physical strength. For example, the crew is required to crank huge winches that raise and lower sails weighing hundreds of pounds. The *Mighty Mary* crew added several women to power positions who did

"Some days, the ocean came alive to inspire terror: every time the boat pounded off a wave, it seemed as if the hull would explode; every time a gust of wind hit, you waited for the sails or the rigging to blow up in your face. With every mood, the feeling of anticipation — of what the next day or the next nightfall would bring — was almost the worst part."

not have a background in sailing. These women included two Olympic rowers and Shelley Beattie, who was better known as Siren on television's *American Gladiators*. But Riley argued that physical strength was not the primary obstacle to her success with *Mighty Mary*. "It's not a strength issue," she stated. "Yes, men are generally stronger than women. But it's a matter of experience, and men had a 100-or-so-year head start on women. Experience isn't something you inherit. You have to do it to earn it."

> "An all-women crew limits your crew to the best from only 10 percent of the sailing population," she noted of her decision to select a co-ed crew for the 1999 America's Cup. "We've proved our point. We can do it. It'd be silly to keep making that point. The next point to prove is that women can be part of a winning crew."

Riley and her crew struggled through the first round of competition to decide who would defend the America's Cup for the United States. Riley and Koch eventually concluded that the *Mighty Mary* needed a more experienced tactician in order to succeed. The best person they could find to fill the position was Dave Dellenbaugh, a man who had served as tactician aboard *America3* in 1992. Riley did not hesitate to add Dellenbaugh, even though the crew would no longer consist of all women. "Basically any time you're not winning, you're always going to look at all your options," she explained. "Dave seemed the logical person to step in." Unfortunately, the lack of experience continued to cost *Mighty Mary*, and Riley's boat ended up losing to Dennis Conner's *Young America* in the semifinals. Conner went on to lose the America's Cup to New Zealand in the finals.

The 1999 America's Cup

Immediately after *Mighty Mary* was eliminated from the America's Cup defender trials, Riley began putting together her own co-ed team for the 1999 event. "An all-women crew limits your crew to the best from only 10 percent of the sailing population," she noted of her decision to select a co-ed crew. "We've proved our point. We can do it. It'd be silly to keep making that point. The next point to prove is that women can be part of a winning crew." In forming her own team, Riley also hoped to prove that a woman could lead an America's Cup effort from start to finish. "Having

The America True *sails in the Hauraki Gulf off Auckland, New Zealand, on its way out to the America's Cup course.*

my own Cup boat was a logical progression," she noted. "What else was there left for me to do?"

Riley formed the *America True* syndicate to raise money to build a boat, hire a crew, and eventually compete for the Cup. Beginning in 1997, she spent much of her time visiting potential corporate sponsors to line up financial support. She drew upon her advertising background in her quest for sponsors. "It's a matter of putting together a Power-Point sales presentation, distributing brochures, making cold calls, closing the deal," she stated. "All it is for me is sharing my passion and hopefully they jump on board." Two of Riley's most important supporters were *America3* owner Bill Koch and Chris Coffin, a sailing fan and inventor of the Palm Pilot.

With input from a team of scientists at the National Aeronautics and Space Administration (NASA), Riley designed and built a state-of-the-art, 75-foot racing sailboat. She also put together the best crew she could find. The complete crew of *America True* included six women.

Since the United States had lost the America's Cup to New Zealand two years earlier, *America True* had to compete against 11 teams from seven different countries to earn the right to face New Zealand in the finals. The challenger races were divided into two rounds of head-to-head competition, with the top six teams from the first round continuing to the second round. Some of the toughest competition included *Young America* of the New York Yacht Club, *AmericaOne* out of San Diego, *Nippon* from Japan, and *Prada* of Italy.

———— **"** ————

"What's happened over the last 10 to 20 years is that we've gone from just a few women in racing to a moderate amount to the point now where almost every guy that's sailing knows at least one girl who's very competitive, very good. The Maiden, that first women's team, gave women the motivation to go sailing, to know that they could do it themselves. That's really when everyone else's attitude started to change."

———— **"** ————

America True surprised many observers by finishing second in the first round, behind the well-funded *Prada* team, to advance to the semifinals of the challenger series. After she had wrapped up second place, Riley created some controversy by declining to compete in the last match race against France. But Riley felt it was more important to use the time to make repairs to her boat. "We have accomplished what we needed to in advancing the boat to the semifinals. I'm sorry to be selfish, but that's what we're here for," she explained. "At some point in the America's Cup you have to look at what's best for your project. We're here as a competitor, not to win a popularity contest."

Unfortunately, *America True* faltered in the semifinals. Riley decided to make some changes to the boat in order to adjust to the light breezes that had dominated the competition. As soon as she made the changes, however, the conditions changed to heavy winds. Italy's *Prada* went on to win the challenger series but then lost to New Zealand in the America's Cup finals.

Although she was disappointed not to make the finals, Riley believed that *America True* had proven that women had a legitimate place in top international sailing competitions. "The success of this program will be to establish women as valuable parts of the team in every aspect—in the administration, in the rigging shop, in the sail loft and on the boat," she stated. "That's when people will stop looking at us like we're some sort of mystery, wondering, 'Who's really pulling the strings?'" In recognition of her efforts, Riley received the 1999 Rolex Yachtswoman of the Year Award.

After *America True* was eliminated, Riley began planning for the next America's Cup race in 2002. She is proud that her various efforts over the years have brought more women into the top levels of sailing. "What's happened over the last 10 to 20 years is that we've gone from just a few women in racing to a moderate amount to the point now where almost every guy that's sailing knows at least one girl who's very competitive, very good," she noted. "The *Maiden,* that first women's team, gave women the motivation to go sailing, to know that they could do it them-selves. That's really when everyone else's attitude started to change."

HOME AND FAMILY

Riley became engaged to Barry McKay, a fellow sailor from New Zealand, in 1993. Immediately after their engagement, Riley took over as captain of the *U.S. Women's Challenge* in the Whitbread Round-the-World Race. When she returned from nearly nine months at sea, they bought a 100-year-old house in Auckland and began fixing it up together. As time passed, however, Riley and McKay found that their busy sailing schedules left them very little time to be together. They finally broke up in 1998. "It just didn't work anymore," Riley explained. "Who knows? Maybe we'll run into each other in Auckland in 2000 and start up again. Or maybe not." When she is not traveling or racing on a sailboat, Riley lives in an apartment in San Francisco, California.

HOBBIES AND OTHER INTERESTS

Riley admits that she has little time to pursue hobbies other than sailing. In her limited time off, she says, "I try to squeeze a date in occasionally. I also like snow skiing. Since I rarely stay in one place long, my activities tend to vary. If I'm in Jamaica, I do more scuba diving. If I'm in Florida, I run on the beach and at night go to clubs along the strip."

Riley shares her passion for sailing with other people as a motivational speaker. She often gives slide presentations based on her adventures at sea to groups from yacht clubs, high schools, girls' clubs, and other orga-nizations. In addition, her America's Cup team, *America True,* sponsors a program called True Youth to introduce at-risk children to sailing. "We are continuing our mission to promote sailing, and introduce children to sail-ing who might not otherwise get out on the water," Riley noted. "This is the fun part."

WRITINGS

Taking the Helm, 1995 (with Cynthia Flanagan)

HONORS AND AWARDS

Michiganian of the Year (*Detroit Free Press*): 1999
Rolex Yachtswoman of the Year: 1999

FURTHER READING

Books

Riley, Dawn, with Cynthia Flanagan. *Taking the Helm,* 1995

Periodicals

Baltimore Sun, Feb. 6, 1994, p.C17
Boston Globe, Aug. 14, 1994, sec. Magazine, p.12; Jan. 1, 2000, p.C1
Chicago Tribune, June 16, 1991, sec. Womanews, p.1
Dallas Morning News, Oct. 20, 1999, p.C5
Detroit News, Dec. 8, 1999, p.E1
Independent (London), May 14, 1994, p.50
Los Angeles Times, Apr. 24, 1991, p.C1; Apr. 16, 1992, p.C7
Ms., Feb.-Mar. 2000, p.25
New York Times, Nov. 15, 1993, p.C2; Jan. 30, 1994, sec. 8, p.8
San Diego Union-Tribune, Feb. 7, 1992, p.D1; June 17, 1994, p.D1; Jan. 1,
    2000, p.D6
San Francisco Chronicle, Nov. 1, 1998, p.Z1; Nov. 15, 1999, p.A1; Dec. 29,
    1999, p.A1
Sports Illustrated, May 9, 1994, p.72; Feb. 20, 1995, p.40; June 14, 1999,
    p.12
USA Today, Nov. 12, 1993, p.C2
Washington Post, Jan. 14, 1990, p.D20; Mar. 7, 1990, p.F2; Nov. 10, 1993,
    p.B1; Nov. 11, 1993, p.B2; Jan. 26, 1994, p.C3; May 26, 1994, p.B3; June
    2, 1999, p.D3; Oct. 24, 1999, p.D3; Jan. 12, 2000, p.D2; Jan. 14, 2000,
    p.D2
Women's Sports and Fitness, May-June 1992, p.106; Sep. 1994, p.22

WORLD WIDE WEB SITE

http://www.americatrue.org

Karen Smyers 1961-

American Triathlete
Five-Time World Champion at the Olympic Triathlon
Distance and Winner of the 1995 Ironman Triathlon

[Editor's note: Karen Smyers kindly agreed to be interviewed for this profile. We thank her for her time and her graciousness.]

BIRTH

Karen Smyers was born on September 1, 1961 in Corry, Pennsylvania. She was one of seven children born to Bill and Mary Anne Smyers. Bill was a civil engineer, and Mary Anne was first a homemaker, and later a computer programmer. They're both retired now. Karen's siblings are sisters Lynn, Donna, Mary, and Laura and brothers Greg and Rick.

YOUTH

When Smyers was a girl, her family moved to Wethersfield, a suburb of Hartford, Connecticut. It was there that she began playing organized sports at the age of eight. She showed great athletic ability, but she had trouble deciding which sport was her favorite. "Ever since I was a kid, I haven't been able to pick one sport," she explained. "It wasn't really a choice to play individual sports, it just ended up that way. I think team sports would have been fun."

"Ever since I was a kid, I haven't been able to pick one sport. It wasn't really a choice to play individual sports, it just ended up that way."

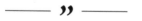

EDUCATION

Smyers took up competitive swimming at the age of 13. As a student at Wethersfield High School, she joined the swim team and tennis team and also participated in gymnastics. Her gymnastics specialty was the vault event. Smyers was an excellent student, and after graduating from high school in 1979, she enrolled at Princeton University in New Jersey. She initially resisted going to the prestigious Ivy League school because she "had the perception of Princeton being very snobby," but she changed her mind after visiting the campus and meeting some of her fellow students.

Princeton offered her a great challenge, academically and athletically. She majored in economics, and she particularly enjoyed her statistics and computer courses. She also spent a good deal of time in the pool. As a member of the Princeton swim team, Smyers spent four to five hours each day swimming. Her events were the 100- and 200-meter breast stroke and the 200- and 400-meter individual medley. This intensive training improved her swimming skills and her overall conditioning, but it also made her realize the importance of taking time off from training. "One year at Princeton, as we got closer to nationals, we began tapering off on our training," she remembered. "In that period, I knocked my time in the 100-yard breaststroke by a couple seconds. That kind of improvement was unheard of, but I know it was the extra month of resting."

Toward the end of her college days, Smyers also began working out with the Princeton track team. On a few occasions, she competed in the half-mile and mile events. She graduated from Princeton with a bachelor's degree in economics in 1983.

CAREER HIGHLIGHTS

The Triathlon

After graduating from college, Smyers took a job with a computer consulting firm in the Boston area. She wanted to continue competing in sports, but she was tired of swimming. "I burned out on swimming after college at Princeton," she admitted, "but I wanted to keep competing at something." One day, her college roommate, Kim Ratcliffe, convinced her to participate in a triathlon. A triathlon is a race that consists of three separate parts: swimming, cycling, and running. The distances vary in different competitions. The type of triathlon Smyers started with is called the "Olympic distance" because the Olympic event is based on it. It consists of a one-mile swim, a 25-mile bike ride, and a 6.2-mile run. Competitors in individual triathlons complete all three parts of the race, in succession, and the triathlete with the fastest combined time wins. To excel in triathlon events, athletes must be skilled at swimming, bicycling, and running, plus have exceptional endurance.

Since Smyers was already an excellent swimmer, she began working on her running and bicycling skills with the help of Ratcliffe. "She was a runner," Smyers explained. "She started doing a couple of triathlons before I ever did. She got me into running. I started running with her as soon as I could keep up. I was biking to and from work, so I tried a couple [triathlons]."

When Smyers entered her first triathlon in 1984, she rode the same old bicycle that she used to commute to work. She quickly learned that she would need better equipment if she hoped to succeed in her new sport. "I was just biking along and I remember these old people going by me and they weren't even trying and I was killing myself," she recalled.

A few months later, Smyers entered another triathlon in Boston. This time, she borrowed a good bike and ended up finishing second. Since it was only her second triathlon, Smyers had registered for the event as an amateur. Afterward, she found out that she would have won $500 for her second-place finish if she had entered as a professional. "It was the last race I entered as an amateur," she stated. The following year, Smyers began to believe that she could become a top triathlete. At the Bay State Triathlon, she passed former Boston Marathon winner Allison Roe in a sprint to the finish line to win the event.

Smyers finishes the swim portion of the triathlon at the Pan Am Games in Winnipeg, Manitoba, Canada, July 24, 1999.

Becoming a World-Class Triathlete

Over the next few years, Smyers continued working at the computer consulting firm. Her training was limited to her spare time. This arrangement proved difficult for her and prevented her from reaching her potential as a triathlete. In 1989, however, the company she worked for went out of business. She decided to take advantage of this development to become a full-time triathlete. "Until that time, I was racing on a part-time basis," she remembered. "I would train when I could and squeeze in a race here and there. When my employer went bankrupt and I lost my job, I decided to go full-time and professional. Losing my job actually gave me much more flexibility. I had time to train and didn't have to worry about arranging my vacation time around the triathlons I wanted to enter."

Smyers's decision paid off in 1990, when she won the world championship in women's triathlon. During the race, Smyers found herself in second place at the beginning of the run. But she soon got passed by two other competitors. Smyers focused on the woman in third place, hoping to catch her in order to finish in the top three. But she ended up catching all three women ahead of her. "I caught up to them with about a half-mile to go," she recalled. "Someone yelled, '800 meters.' I just said, 'Now or never.' I just started sprinting. They were tired, and they couldn't go with me."

This victory made Smyers the top-ranked female triathlete in the world, only one year after she began training full-time. She also won the first of five consecutive U.S. national championships in 1990. Competing at such a high level, Smyers found that she was able to make a good living as a professional triathlete. Her income came from prize money and endorsement deals with shoe, sportswear, and bike companies. She managed to top her breakout performance in 1992. She won 15 of the 19 triathlons she entered, including an amazing streak of 11 victories in a row, and claimed $50,000 in prize money. In recognition of her efforts, *Triathlete Magazine* named her Triathlete of the Year.

The Ironman Triathlon

The distances for the triathlons Smyers usually competed in—a 1 mile swim, 25 mile bike, and 6.2 mile run—are the generally accepted distances for international competition. But probably the most famous triathlon event, the Ironman Triathlon, featured much longer distances. Held every year in Hawaii, the Ironman includes a 2.4-mile swim, 112-mile bike ride, and 26.2-mile run. It is considered one of the most grueling endurance competitions in the world. The top competitors usually take eight to nine hours to complete the event.

The first time Smyers ever heard about the Ironman Triathlon, her reaction was to call it "pretty loony." She often said that she would never consider participating in the Ironman, even though it was the best-known event in her sport. "It's too much training and those distances just aren't my cup of tea," she explained. "I want to keep my races fun. I don't want to have to train myself to death." But in 1993, she made a deal with her husband, Michael King. He announced that he was going to try to qualify for the famous race as an amateur. Smyers said that if he qualified, she would also compete in the race as a professional. Both of them ended up participating in the Ironman Triathlon that year. Smyers finished fourth among all women competitors and posted the best time ever for a first-time woman participant. Despite all the praise she received for her awesome athletic achievement, Smyers was practical and objective about her abilities. "I hate to burst anyone's bubble," she said, but I'm no bionic woman. You don't have to be Superwoman to do this. All you have to be is balanced. And you can't have a weakness."

In 1994, Smyers competed in the Ironman again and finished second to legendary triathlete Paula Newby Fraser, who won the event a remarkable seven times. The following year, Fraser announced that the 1995 race would be her final Ironman event. Knowing that it would be her last chance to beat Fraser, Smyers entered too. The race turned into a showdown between the two competitors. Smyers finished the swim portion even with Fraser, but Fraser built an impressive 12-minute lead in the bike portion. During the marathon-length run, Smyers gradually cut Fraser's lead to three minutes at the 21-mile mark. Upon learning that Smyers was drawing closer, Fraser decided to quit taking water breaks in order to save time. But this ended up being a crucial error for the defending champion.

> "I hate to burst anyone's bubble, but I'm no bionic woman. You don't have to be Superwoman to do this. All you have to be is balanced. And you can't have a weakness."

Within sight of the finish line, Smyers caught up to Fraser. "Her face looked kind of blank," Smyers noted. "I remember thinking something was wrong with her." Sure enough, Fraser began stumbling and collapsed from dehydration. Smyers went on to win the race, while Fraser recovered several minutes later to finish fourth. Some observers claimed that Smyers would not have won if Fraser had not collapsed. But her fellow competitors argued that Fraser would not have collapsed if Smyers had not pushed her beyond the limit of her abilities. After all, Smyers had won the race by posting the second-fastest marathon run by a woman in Ironman history.

By winning the 1995 Ironman Triathlon, Smyers proved that she could be a dominant force in her sport at any distance. Just one month later, she won another women's triathlon world championship at the Olympic dis-

Smyers competes in the cycling portion of the triathlon at the Pan Am Games in Winnipeg, Manitoba, Canada, July 24, 1999.

tance. Many people were amazed that she could recover from the grueling Ironman in time to compete in the world championships, let alone win the race against the top international competitors. In fact, Smyers became the only person ever to accomplish the two feats in the same year.

Her spectacular 1995 season earned her Triathlete of the Year honors from *Triathlete Magazine* for the second time in her career.

Serious Injuries

In 1997, just as she reached the peak of her career, Smyers suffered the first in a series of setbacks that kept her out of competition for most of two years. This string of misfortunes began with a freak accident at her home. As she was removing a storm window, she dropped it and the glass shattered. A piece of glass became lodged in the back of her leg and severed her hamstring muscle. She had emergency surgery to repair the damage.

Knowing that she had to take six months off for her injury to heal, Smyers decided to use the time to start a family. She and her husband had discussed having children for several years, but they kept waiting for the right time. "It's very hard when you feel you're in the best shape of your life to voluntarily take time off and put on 25 or 30 pounds and completely change your body and not know if it's going to come back the way it was," she explained. Smyers continued running until five weeks before her baby was due, and she swam and lifted weights up until the end of her pregnancy. She gave birth to a daughter, Jenna, by caesarean section in May 1998. Smyers returned to training a few weeks later.

"I started this sport in 1984, in the early days. The Olympics was always a dream that the sport had. I've been waiting for this day to roll around for a long time."

That August—just three months after giving birth—Smyers competed in the triathlon at the Goodwill Games. Despite her long layoff from competition, she was disappointed with her finish of 22nd place. "I had every reason not to be competitive at the Goodwill Games, but even so I went there thinking I could probably rise to the occasion and at least not embarrass myself," she noted. "Yet I felt like I had embarrassed myself."

But Smyers continued training. She was determined to regain her previous form and return to the top of the triathlon rankings. Then another disaster struck. During a training ride on her bike, she was clipped by the back of an 18-wheel truck as it tried to pass her on a winding road. Smyers fell off her bike and skidded 60 feet down the road into a stone wall. Immediately after the accident, her training partner used his cellular phone to call her husband. But King was busy feeding their baby and could not answer the phone. Instead, he heard a frightening message on the answering machine. "The voice was almost frantic," King remembered. "'Michael, Michael, pick up the telephone.' Then all of a sudden he said, 'Karen, don't move' and 'I'll have to call you back.'"

Smyers suffered six broken ribs, a separated shoulder, and a bruised lung in the accident. She recovered physically and was able to begin swimming again within a few weeks. But she still feels the effects of the crash emotionally. In fact, she has to fight the urge to pull her bike off the road whenever she hears a truck approaching from behind. "It's like an involuntary reaction when I hear a motor behind me," she admitted. "My stomach just goes into knots and I start to shake."

Olympic Dreams

Between surgery and childbirth and the accident, Smyers was sidelined for two years at a time when she was at the top of her sport. But the layoffs only made her more determined to continue training in order to compete in the 2000 Olympic Games in Sydney, Australia, which would feature the triathlon as a medal sport for the first time. "Making the Olympic team is the biggest thing on my mind," she stated. "I started this sport in 1984, in the early days. The Olympics was always a dream that the sport had. I've been waiting for this day to roll around for a long time."

"As a mom, my first priority is getting better for the long term," she said after her cancer diagnosis. "I've done more in the sport than I ever dreamed of. I could retire tomorrow and still be completely satisfied with my career."

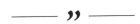

In 1999, Smyers represented the United States at the Pan Am Games. She was honored when her fellow athletes selected her to carry the American flag in the opening ceremonies. She finished seventh in the triathlon at the Pan Am Games. She felt confident about her chances of making the U.S. Olympic triathlon team at the tryouts in the spring of 2000.

A Diagnosis of Cancer

Unfortunately, Smyers encountered yet another setback on her road to the Olympics. In October 1999, she was diagnosed with thyroid cancer. The thyroid is a gland in the neck that produces hormones, special chemicals that regulate bodily functions like heart rate, body temperature, and blood pressure. Despite the diagnosis, Smyers decided to go ahead and compete in the 1999 Ironman, where she finished second. She also competed in a triathlon in Mexico, where she collided with another competitor on her bike and broke her collarbone. She had surgery to remove her thyroid gland and two lymph nodes shortly before Christmas. She also began taking artificial hormones to replace the ones that were formerly produced by her thyroid. "There were some scary moments," she recalled. "Probably the scariest is when that c-word was mentioned for the first time. Now I'm feeling fine. One thing I've learned the last couple of years is how incredible the human body is in recovering from things."

—————— " ——————

Smyers, who was in labor for 48 hours with Jenna, claims that having a baby is harder than competing in the Ironman triathlon. "Only a small percentage of people in the world can do the Ironman," she noted. "Fifty percent of the people can do labor, and let me tell you, labor is harder. You don't have a choice when you go into labor. You can't drop out."

—————— " ——————

On the positive side, thyroid cancer is highly curable. It tends to grow very slowly, and it rarely spreads to other parts of the body. The usual treatment for thyroid cancer is surgery, followed by therapy with radioactive iodine. Smyers's doctors assured her that she could delay the second part of her treatment until after the Olympic trials. She emphasized that she would not have considered delaying the radioactive iodine therapy if there was any risk to her health. And her experiences have made her priorities clear. "As a mom, my first priority is getting better for the long term," she stated. "I've done more in the sport than I ever dreamed of. I could retire tomorrow and still be completely satisfied with my career."

Smyers had two opportunities to make the U.S. Olympic triathlon team. The first was a race in Sydney, Australia, in April 2000. Unfortunately, she failed to finish in the top ten in that event. Jennifer Gutierrez, the top American finisher, received the first spot on the Olympic team. Smyers's next chance came at the U.S. national championships on May 27, 2000, where the top two finishers qualified for the Olympics. Smyers finished seventh in the competition, less than two minutes after the top finishers. While she won't be representing the U.S. in the Olympics, she is looking forward to competing in the Ironman in October 2000, when her cancer treatments will be over.

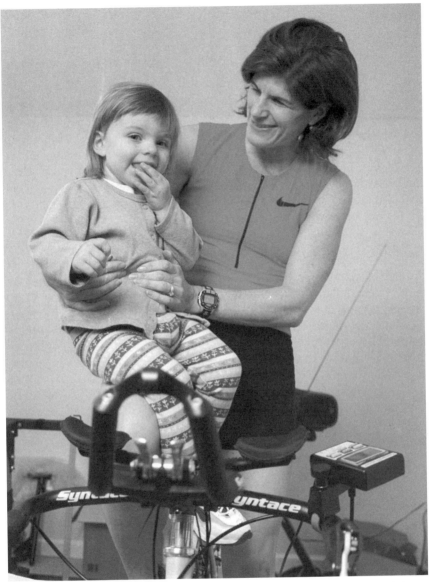

Smyers holds her daughter, Jenna, on a stationary bike as she takes a break from training at her Lincoln, Mass. home.

After the race, Smyers said she hoped she hadn't let down her many supporters. "I was just hoping they didn't get carried away with the hype I was getting before the race. I just tried to get every ounce out of my body that I could all the way to the very end, and I think I did that."

135

Although her quest for Olympic gold is over, Smyers has already secured a place as one of the best female triathletes in the history of the sport. "I sometimes just pinch myself and say I can't believe that this is the way I'm actually making a living," she noted. "To be paid for staying in shape and getting better at swimming, biking, and running, is like a dream."

Despite the intensity she shows in competition and the serious challenges to her health over the past few years, Smyers remains a warm, laid-back person with a wonderful sense of humor. In her column in *Inside Triathlon* magazine, she joked that "After the radioactive iodine treatment, I will be able to read in bed without a night light and go for a run without reflective clothing." And her sense of humor helps her to put everything in perspective. "The last two years were pretty good," she says wryly, "except for the broken bones and cancer."

MARRIAGE AND FAMILY

Karen Smyers lives with her family in Lincoln, Massachusetts. Her husband, Michael King, once owned a bar and is now an independent film producer. They married in 1992 and their daughter, Jenna Smyers King, was born on May 1, 1998. Smyers, who was in labor for 48 hours with Jenna, claims that having a baby is harder than competing in the Ironman triathlon. "Only a small percentage of people in the world can do the Ironman," she noted. "Fifty percent of the people can do labor, and let me tell you, labor is harder. You don't have a choice when you go into labor. You can't drop out."

WRITINGS

Triathlon 101: Essentials for Multisport Success, 1999 (with John M. Mora)

Smyers also writes a regular column for *Inside Triathlon* magazine.

HONORS AND AWARDS

Triathlon National Champion: 1990-95
Triathlon World Champion: 1990, 1992, 1995
Triathlete of the Year (*Triathlete Magazine*): 1992, 1995

FURTHER READING

Periodicals

Boston Globe, Oct. 10, 1990, p.59; Feb. 9, 1992, sec. Northwest Weekly, p.1; Sep. 16, 1994, sec. Sports, p.99; Oct. 25, 1996, p.E1; July 21, 1999, p.C1; Jan. 20, 2000, p.C2

Chicago Tribune, July 24, 1999, sec. Sports, p.4
Cleveland Plain Dealer, July 18, 1996, p.D10
Dallas Morning News, Jan. 22, 2000, p.B11
New York Daily News, July 26, 1998, p.93
New York Times, Jan. 21, 2000, p.C5
Philadelphia Inquirer, Aug. 2, 1999, Section: Sports, p.1
Sports Illustrated, May 1, 2000, p.83
St. Peterburg Times, Apr. 23, 1997, p.C3; Apr. 24, 1999, p.C1
USA Today, Jan. 19, 2000, p.C8
Washington Post, Apr. 15, 2000, p.D1
Women's Sports and Fitness, Sep. 1992, p.78

OTHER

"Morning Edition"Transcript, National Public Radio, Oct. 6, 1994; "All Things Considered"Transcript, Mar. 23, 2000

ADDRESS

USA Triathlon
3595 E. Fountain Dr,
Suite 711
Colorado Springs, CO 80910

WORLD WIDE WEB SITE

http://insidetri.com

Kurt Warner 1971-

American Professional Football Player with the St. Louis Rams
Starting Quarterback of the 1999 Super Bowl Champions

BIRTH

Kurtis Eugene Warner was born on June 22, 1971, in Burlington, Iowa. He was the second son of Gene Warner, a phone company supervisor, and Sue Warner, a clerk for a plastic bag manufacturer. His parents divorced when Kurt was five years old. He and his brother, Matt, who is 15 months older, were raised by their mother in Cedar Rapids, Iowa. On weekends, they visited their father, his second wife, Mimi, and their stepbrother, Matt Post.

YOUTH

Both Gene and Sue Warner were strict parents who raised their boys to be respectful and obedient. In fact, they sometimes swatted Kurt on the back of the legs with a wooden spoon to keep him in line. As a devoted single mother who worked three jobs to take care of her family, Sue Warner believed that discipline was important. "I've always known that you create your own monsters," she said, "and I didn't want my kids to grow up to be people I didn't like. I mean, I would always love them, but I wanted to like them as human beings and people."

For the most part, Kurt was a well-behaved boy. But he did occasionally get into some harmless mischief. For example, his mother remembered that he used to ring neighbors' doorbells and then run away. For a few years, Sue Warner referred to her son as "Dennis the Menace" because of the chaos he created around the house. He often did things like take all the sheets off the clothesline to use as capes in a game with his friends. Once, he put light bulbs in the dryer with a load of laundry.

One of Kurt's frequent problems as a child was getting lost in the super-market. "I wouldn't be in there two minutes when I would hear Kurt's lit-tle voice on their public address system and 'would the mother of Kurt Warner please come get her boy? He's lost,'" his mother recalled. "I finally got to the point where I decided he wasn't lost, he just wanted to hear his name over the loudspeaker."

EDUCATION

Warner went to elementary school at All-Saints Catholic School in Cedar Rapids. He excelled in all sports while he was growing up, and in the eighth grade he became a starter on the school basketball team. The fol-lowing year, he went on to Cedar Rapids Regis High School, where he lettered in football, basketball, and baseball. Warner tried out for the var-sity football team his freshman year as a wide receiver, but he was moved to quarterback once his coach saw him throw the football. While at Regis High, he passed for more than 1,500 yards with a completion rate of 60 percent. He received all-state honors in his senior year, and his team made the playoffs with a 7-2 record. His coach, Gaylord Hauschildt, al-ways knew that the young quarterback was special. "If you wanted a mold where you could create successful young people, you would mold it around Kurt Warner," he stated.

Like millions of other kids, Warner dreamed of becoming a professional athlete someday. As he developed through high school, it became apparent that his size (six feet, two inches tall and 215 pounds) and skills were best suited to football. But despite Warner's strong arm, intelligence, and willingness to work hard, college recruiters were not overly impressed with him. After graduating from Cedar Rapids Regis in 1989, he received only one offer of a partial scholarship to play football at Northern Iowa University. This was the beginning of a pattern—no one saw Warner's full potential except Kurt himself.

> *One of Kurt's frequent problems as a child was getting lost in the supermarket. "I wouldn't be in there two minutes when I would hear Kurt's little voice on their public address system and 'would the mother of Kurt Warner please come get her boy? He's lost,'" his mother recalled. "I finally got to the point where I decided he wasn't lost, he just wanted to hear his name over the loudspeaker."*

CAREER HIGHLIGHTS

College Football—Northern Iowa

Despite the fact that Northern Iowa was a Division I-AA school—meaning that it was a smaller school with a less prominent athletic program than those found at the nation's largest colleges—Warner accepted the scholarship offer. After all, Northern Iowa was the only university to give him a chance to play the sport he loved. But things didn't get any easier for him at the college level. Warner rode the bench for the first three years under coach Terry Allen. "I guess you could say that I was as responsible for holding him back as anyone," Allen admitted. "I made him sit the bench for three years."

Warner nearly quit the team during his junior year, in 1992. The coach promised him that he would play in the game against McNeese State, but it didn't happen. Angry and disappointed, Warner called his father and told him he wanted to quit. But Gene Warner convinced his son to stick it out for his senior season. In 1993, Warner finally got his chance to shine. He threw for over 2,700 yards that season and led his team to the NCAA Division I-AA playoffs. After earning All-Gateway Conference honors for his performance, Warner even thought he might attract some interest from NFL teams. He also graduated that year with a bachelor's degree in communications. It seemed like things were coming together for him. As it turned out, however, there were many more bumps on his road to the top.

A Tryout for the Green Bay Packers

Warner wasn't part of the NFL draft in 1994 — he wasn't good enough to be scouted by the NFL, and no teams were interested in him. But he did get a chance to tryout for the Green Bay Packers, and he thought he might achieve his dream of playing in the NFL. Warner had to compete against Brett Favre, the Packers' star quarterback; former collegiate Heisman Trophy winner Ty Detmer; and promising newcomer Mark Brunell, who later went on to fame with the Jacksonville Jaguars. Warner wasn't as flashy as most of the pro players, and he sometimes struggled to fit in. In fact, Favre gave him the nickname Potsie (from the nerdy character on the old television show *Happy Days*). This pressure, combined with the stiff competition for the quarterback job, made his task almost impossible.

Warner didn't make the Packers team. This setback was a tremendous disappointment to the young quarterback. After all, his only desire was to support himself by playing a sport that he loved. When the Packers cut him from the team, Warner returned home to Iowa, where he took a job as a stock boy for a grocery chain. But he refused to give up his dream of playing professional football. It was difficult not to give up hope, since the prospect of getting another tryout with an NFL team seemed remote. But Warner worked at night and continued training and studying game films during the day. He also got a little practice by tossing bags of candy over shelves to other employees and throwing Nerf footballs when no one was around. He wanted to be sure he was ready when the next opportunity came along.

Arena Football — Iowa Barnstormers

In 1995, Warner was hired by John Gregory, the head coach of a new Arena Football League Team called the Iowa Barnstormers. Arena football is played indoors on a much smaller field than the ones used in college and the NFL. In addition, each team puts eight players on the field rather than 11. Otherwise, the rules are similar to regular football. Arena games are often wild, high-scoring affairs with an emphasis on passing. Although playing with the Barnstormers was not Warner's dream job, he was pleased to be back playing football.

Warner rolls away from Minnesota Vikings pressure during the fourth quarter of the NFC divisional playoff game, January 16, 2000.

In his first game, Warner threw two interceptions and completed only 6 of 13 passes. He improved slowly throughout the season, however, and the Barnstormers finished with a 7-5 record and made the playoffs. Still, the pressure stayed on Warner. Even his teammates underestimated him. "I didn't think there was any hope for him," his former teammate Willis Jacox admitted. "John [Gregory] and I would get into yelling fits with each other about Kurt. John kept on saying that I had to give Kurt time to develop and I wanted to get rid of him." As it turned out, the coach was right. Warner led the Barnstormers to the Arena Bowl championship game the next two years.

Warner finished his Arena football career in 1997 with 10,464 yards passing and 183 touchdowns. Although the statistics really can't be compared to NFL numbers because of the different rules and level of competition, a few people began to take notice of the young quarterback. Playing on a smaller field and reacting quickly to defenses helped Warner develop his game intelligence and improve his release of the ball. By the end of his three-year Arena football career, he was more mature and ready for a second chance in the NFL.

In 1997, Warner thought his big break had come. He was invited to try out for the Chicago Bears. But once again, luck was not on his side. A few weeks before his scheduled tryout, Warner married Brenda Meoni. During their honeymoon in the Caribbean, he was bitten on the elbow of his throwing arm by a spider. The painful bite made it impossible for him to throw effectively, so he had to cancel his tryout.

European Football — Amsterdam Admirals

But a short time later, Warner received a call from Al Luginbill, head coach for the Amsterdam Admirals in NFL Europe (a proving ground for developing NFL talent). Luginbill was familiar with the quarterback's success in the Arena League and asked Warner to join his team. But Warner refused to sign a contract unless an NFL team signed him and then allocated him to the European

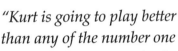

"Kurt is going to play better than any of the number one draft picks at quarterback this year," Coach Dick Vermeil predicted about the 1999 season.

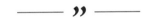

league. Luginbill contacted 12 NFL teams about the deal but couldn't find one that was interested. Finally, the St. Louis Rams—the 13th team— agreed to sign Warner. The main reason was that the personnel director for the St. Louis Rams, Charley Armey, knew Mike Kolling, who was a coach at Northern Iowa. "[Kolling] told me to take a chance on [Kurt]," Armey related. "Obviously, that was some good advice." Warner chose number 13 for his uniform because it took that many teams for him to get a new opportunity to play.

Warner played for the Admirals during the 1998 season, leading them to a winning record and a playoff appearance. He proved himself by leading the league in passing yardage, attempts, completions, and touchdowns. As the 1998 NFL season was getting started, the Rams brought Warner to St. Louis for training camp. It finally looked like he would get another shot at his dream.

In the NFL at Last — St. Louis Rams

With the support of Armey and Coach Dick Vermeil, Warner made the Rams roster as a third-string quarterback. He spent most of the 1998 season pacing the sidelines with a clipboard while veteran quarterback Steve Bono was on the field. Warner's first NFL appearance came at the end of the year in a game against San Francisco. It was not a great outing, as he threw for a total of 39 yards.

The formerly unwanted quarterback was named MVP of both the Super Bowl and the NFL, an honor only five others have achieved. But Warner insisted on sharing the honors with his teammates. "We've had different guys step up and be the MVP of each football game," he stated. "I accept this [award] as something we have earned as a team. To me, this is a team award."

The Rams were a terrible disappointment during the 1998 season. It seemed that the team was falling apart. In fact, there were rumors that Coach Vermeil might be fired. Vermeil was one of Warner's biggest supporters, so the possibility of him leaving the organization was a threat to Warner's future in the NFL. But Rams President Jim Shaw decided to stick with Vermeil for one more year.

As the 1999 season approached, Warner impressed the coaches enough in training camp to earn the second-string spot. Warner was still a backup, but the coaches noticed that he was often effective in running the scout team offense against the first string defense in practice. Vermeil gradually gained confidence in Warner. When starting quarterback Trent Green suffered a preseason knee injury, some members of the Rams organization wanted to bring in a veteran quarterback. But Vermeil insisted on letting Warner play. "Kurt is going to play better than any of the number one draft picks at quarterback this year," Vermeil said.

The 1999 Season and the Super Bowl

Warner rewarded his coach's decision by leading the Rams to tremendous success that year. He started out hot, becoming the only starting quarterback in NFL history to throw for three touchdowns in his first three games. The success continued throughout the season, as Warner routinely

Warner (13) is sacked in the second quarter of Super Bowl XXXIV,
January 30, 2000.

torched opposing defenses with a barrage of touchdown passes. He
ended up completing 325 passes in 499 attempts for 4,353 yards on the
season. He also threw for 41 touchdowns and only 13 interceptions.

With his remarkable performance, Warner lead the Rams to a 13-3 record
and the third most productive offense in NFL history. The Rams struggled
in the first round of the playoffs against the Tampa Bay Buccaneers, but
managed to pull out a victory. In the conference championship game,
they scored 49 points in an impressive win over the powerful Minnesota
Vikings. In just his first year as a starting quarterback, Warner would be
playing in the Super Bowl against the Tennessee Titans.

Warner topped off his amazing season with a record-breaking performance in Super Bowl XXXIV. He passed for 414 yards, beating the previous record of 357 yards set by Hall of Famer Joe Montana in 1989. Warner drove his team down the field to take the lead with 1:54 left on the clock. Then, on the last play of the game, the Rams stopped the Titans on the one yard line in one of the most exciting Super Bowl finishes ever. St. Louis became the champions with a 23-16 victory. The formerly unwanted quarterback was named MVP of both the Super Bowl and the NFL, an honor only five others have achieved. But Warner insisted on sharing the honors with his teammates. "We've had different guys step up and be the MVP of each football game," he stated. "I accept this [award] as something we have earned as a team. To me, this is a team award."

Because of the unusual way he joined the team, Warner played the 1999 season for the league minimum salary of $254,000. This is a tiny sum compared to the salaries of many quarterbacks, some of whom make millions of dollars a year. To show their gratitude to Warner for his role in their success, the Rams paid him $500,000.

Warner became a national star as the media and fans became fascinated by the amazing story of Warner's career. Only five years earlier, the Super Bowl MVP quarterback had been stocking grocery store shelves in Iowa with no prospect of playing pro football. Even opposing players had to respect Warner's fight to overcome the odds. "The man obviously didn't take the elevator to get here," said Carolina Panthers linebacker Kevin Greene. "He took the stairs. And he started at the very bottom of the staircase. Then they put him in the basement, and he still came back up. So you've got to say, 'Hat's off to the guy.'" Throughout the difficult times,

———— " ————

"The man obviously didn't take the elevator to get here," said Carolina Panthers linebacker Kevin Greene. "He took the stairs. And he started at the very bottom of the staircase. Then they put him in the basement, and he still came back up. So you've got to say, 'Hat's off to the guy.'" Throughout the difficult times, Warner never stopped believing in himself. "If anybody tells you you can't do something, don't believe them," he stated. "With a deep faith in yourself, and the good Lord, everything is possible."

———— " ————

Warner holds up the Super Bowl trophy after the Rams defeated the Tennessee Titans, 23-16, in Super Bowl XXXIV, January 30, 2000.

Warner never stopped believing in himself. "If anybody tells you you can't do something, don't believe them," he stated. "With a deep faith in yourself, and the good Lord, everything is possible."

*Warner holds his 10-year-old son, Zachary, who is blind, while taking part in
activities with other visually impaired children at the Delta Gamma Center
in St. Louis, October 19, 1999.*

MARRIAGE AND FAMILY

Kurt Warner met Brenda Meoni in 1993, the same year he became the
starting quarterback at Northern Iowa. They met in a country-western bar
on a night when they both had intended to stay home. At that time,
Brenda was a single mother relying on food stamps to care for her two
children, daughter, Jesse and son, Zachary. Zachary had suffered brain
damage in infancy and is blind. Kurt was only 23 years old at the time;
Brenda was 27. It didn't seem that they would be a likely match, but she
reminded Kurt of someone very special to him. "I really saw a lot of my
mom in [Brenda]," he recalled. "She was a strong woman who was doing
the best she could in a difficult situation." They were married in 1997, and
Kurt legally adopted Jesse and Zachary. The following year, they had a son,
Kade.

For Warner, the most important thing in life is family: "My kids mean the world to me," he noted. "[Zachary is] the most special child I've ever met. The things he goes through on a daily basis, everything is a struggle for him, and you know, for me to go throw three interceptions on a football field and get down on myself and to worry about that is a joke because his life is so difficult. He just gives me a humbling sense and a sense of what's really important in life. I could come home every day and not worry about what people think from the standpoint of I didn't play very well . . . and I know that my family is going to be there loving me. I'm just Dad, and to me that's the most important thing."

Warner also relies on his religious faith to help him through difficult times. Raised as a Catholic, he later converted to Brenda's born-again Christian faith. He believes that God has been essential to his success. "I looked to the Lord a lot and drew a lot of strength from him, knowing that no matter what I faced that he was going to help me through it," he stated. Warner often takes advantage of the exposure he receives as a famous football player to share his religious beliefs with others. He leads Bible studies with his Rams teammates, and he prays on the field after games. He also uses every available opportunity available to mention God's importance in his life. "If I can reach just one person," he said, "I know that is what Christ wants me to do."

HOBBIES AND OTHER INTERESTS

In his limited spare time, Warner's favorite thing is being with his family. He likes to nap with Kade. He also wrestles with Zachary and spends at least one evening a week

> *For Warner, the most important thing in life is family. "My kids mean the world to me," he noted. "[Zachary is] the most special child I've ever met. The things he goes through on a daily basis, everything is a struggle for him, and you know, for me to go throw three interceptions on a football field and get down on myself and to worry about that is a joke because his life is so difficult. He just gives me a humbling sense and a sense of what's really important in life . . . and I know that my family is going to be there loving me. I'm just Dad, and to me that's the most important thing."*

Warner, with wife Brenda, waves to the media while holding son Kade.

with his Jesse. He sometimes goes hunting and fishing with his father, but he spends most of his time off at home watching TV or listening to the radio. Warner is also active in charity work. He volunteers his time at Camp Barnabas in Missouri, which helps needy children, and at the St. Louis Family Church. He also raises money for charity through sales of his own brand of cereal, called "Warner's Crunch Time." Warner also works with charities to held disabled children, like Zachary.

HONORS AND AWARDS

NFL Player of the Month: October 1999
Miller Lite Player of the Year: 1999
NFL Most Valuable Player: 1999
Super Bowl XXXIV Most Valuable Player: 1999
NFL Pro Bowl: 1999

FURTHER READING

Books

Balzer, Howard. *Kurt Warner: The Quarterback,* 2000 (juvenile)

Periodicals

Boston Globe, Jan. 16, 2000, p. D1; Jan. 31, 2000, p.D1
Chicago Tribune, Jan. 19, 2000, p.2
Des Moines Register, Dec. 5, 1999, p.1; Jan. 30, 2000, p.1
People, Jan. 17, 2000, p.99
St. Louis Post Dispatch, Aug. 26, 1998, p.D1; Oct. 4, 1999, p.F1; Dec. 2,
    1999, p.B1; Jan. 7, 2000, p.D8; Jan. 23, 2000, p.F26; Jan. 26, 2000, p.B1;
    Feb. 2, 2000, p.D3
San Francisco Chronicle, Oct. 9, 1999, p.E7; Jan. 22, 2000, p.D1; Jan. 27,
    2000, p.D1; Jan. 31, 2000, p.E1
Sports Illustrated, Sep. 13, 1999, p.112; Oct. 18, 1999, p.58
Sporting News, Oct. 18, 1999, p.22
USA Today, Jan. 26, 2000, p.C1

ADDRESS

St. Louis Rams Football Club
One Rams Way
St. Louis, MO 63045

WORLD WIDE WEB SITES

http://www.stlouisrams.com
http://www.nfl.com/players/profile/3611.html

Serena Williams 1981-
American Professional Tennis Player
Winner of the 1999 U.S. Open

BIRTH

Serena Williams was born on September 26, 1981, in Saginaw, Michigan. She was the youngest of five children, all of them girls, born to Richard and Oracene (Price) Williams. Her father was an entrepreneur who ran several of his own businesses, including a security company and a charter bus service. Her mother once worked as a nurse. Her sisters are Yetunde, Isha, Lyndrea, and Venus. Venus, who is only 15 months older than Serena, is also a professional tennis player. Both parents are now involved in managing their tennis careers.

YOUTH

Serena's life in the world of tennis was planned even before she was born. One day, her father was watching television and saw a woman receive a check for $30,000 for winning a tennis tournament. He decided at that moment that he would make his daughters into great tennis players so they could win a lot of money. He taught himself to play tennis by reading books and magazines and watching tennis instruction videos. Then he began working with his children. Although the entire Williams family learned to play tennis, it was the two youngest daughters who really took to the game. "We had a long-term plan and a work ethic," Richard Williams explained. "I taught my children that they were the very best, and they believed it."

Serena grew up in Compton, California, a poor city south of Los Angeles that suffers from high levels of crime. She started playing tennis on the cracked and trash-strewn public tennis courts there when she was about five years old. Her dad would take her and her sister Venus out to the courts with a shopping cart full of tennis balls and work with them every day. Soon, both girls' natural talents became apparent. Their father began entering them in state tennis tournaments. Serena won her first tournament when she was nine years old. Before long, she and her sister rose to the top of the California junior tennis circuit.

But as the Williams sisters showed the potential to be tennis stars, Richard Williams became alarmed at the amount of attention they received from fans and sports agents. He did not want his daughters to be distracted from their training or their education, so he made the unusual decision to hold them out of junior tournaments. Some people in the tennis community criticized his decision. They claimed that Serena and Venus would never improve their skills beyond a certain point if they did not play against top-level players in a competitive atmosphere. But other people supported Richard Williams's decision to bring his daughters along slowly. They pointed out that several other teenage tennis stars of previous years had struggled to deal with the pressures of turning pro too early.

EDUCATION

Serena received much of her early education at home from her mother, who has a college degree in education. When she was 10 years old, her

family moved to Palm Beach Gardens, Florida, so that she and Venus could attend a private tennis academy. From 1991 to 1995, they practiced tennis and completed their lessons at this school. Later, Serena attended the Driftwood Academy, a 30-student private high school in Lake Park, Florida. She graduated in August 1998.

In between her professional tennis matches, Serena has been taking college courses toward a degree in fashion design. "I like clothes," she explained. "I guess it's because there are so many things you can do to express yourself." Her father always emphasized the importance of education and pushed his daughters to have a career plan for after tennis. "I've told the girls they aren't leaving education behind for tennis," Richard Williams stated. "And I don't necessarily mean school education. . . . So many times you see a great athlete at the end of their career, and they're sitting around saying, 'Look who I once was.' They're just a bunch of damn fools with nothing to fall back on."

CAREER HIGHLIGHTS

Speedy Climb Up the Ranks

In October 1995, when Serena was 14, her father decided that she was ready to play her first professional tennis match. Unfortunately, she lost by a lopsided score of 6-1, 6-1. (In women's tennis, a player wins a match by defeating her opponent in 2 out of 3 sets. The first player to win 6 games usually wins the set, but if their margin of victory is less than 2 games, the set is decided by a tie-breaker. Shorthand notation is often used to show the score of a tennis match. For example, 6-2, 4-6, 7-6 means that the player in question won the first set by a score of 6 games to 2, lost the next set 4 games to 6, and came back to win the match in a third-set tie-breaker.)

Williams played no matches in 1996. Instead, she concentrated on improving her game.. In 1997, she joined the Women's Tennis Association (WTA) professional tour. Her powerful all-around game, highlighted by first serves that regularly reach speeds of 110 miles per hour, helped her make an immediate mark in women's tennis. Williams entered the Ameritech Cup—her second WTA tour event, and the fifth professional tournament of her career—ranked as the 304th best female player in the world. But in her second round match, Williams defeated the seventh-ranked woman in the world, Mary Pierce. And then, as if beating one player in the top ten wasn't enough, she beat fourth-ranked Monica Seles in the quarterfinals. Following this tournament, Williams's world ranking jumped from 304 to 102. "I think I've emerged," she stated afterward.

Williams continued to surprise higher-ranked competitors in her next WTA tour event in 1998. At a tournament in Sydney, Australia, she made a brilliant comeback to defeat the second-ranked woman in the world, Lindsay Davenport. Later that year, she made another impressive showing at the prestigious Lipton Championship, beating three players ranked in the top 30 in the world. She also had a match point (one point away from victory) against the top player in the world, Martina Hingis, before losing to her in three sets. After playing only 16 matches on the WTA Tour, Williams's ranking had climbed to number 30 in the world.

First Grand Slam Singles Event

As one of the top-ranked professional players, Williams was allowed to enter her first Grand Slam singles event, the Australian Open, in 1998.

"Family comes first, no matter how many times we play each other," Serena explained about her relationship with her sister Venus. "Nothing will come between me and my sister."

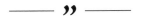

(The four biggest events in tennis—the Australian Open, the French Open, the U.S. Open, and Wimbledon—are known as the Grand Slam.) "I'm just so happy that I'm in the Australian Open," she said upon arriving at the event. Unfortunately, Serena lost in the second round to her big sister, Venus.

The rest of 1998 held some difficult times for Serena, as well as some high points. At Wimbledon, for example, she retired from her third-round match, claiming she had strained a muscle and could not go on. But some observers felt that she was being a poor loser. She was losing the match 7-5, 4-1 at the time she quit, and she did not shake her opponent's hand afterward. The final handshake is a time-honored tradition in tennis and a symbol of the good sportsmanship demanded of all players. Critics also pointed out that the injury was not serious enough to prevent Williams from playing in the mixed doubles event at Wimbledon. She and her partner, Max Mirnyi of Belarus, won the title. Later that year, the team of Williams and Mirnyi also won the U.S. Open mixed doubles title.

First Singles Title

Williams's rise to the top ranks of women's tennis continued in 1999, when she won her first WTA singles title at the Open Gaz de France in Paris. She defeated Amelie Mauresmo in the finals by a score of 6-2, 3-6,

Serena Williams and Venus Williams (foreground) competing in the French Open women's doubles final, June 6, 1999. The Williams sisters won the match.

7-6. Williams followed this success with another win only a week later at the Evert Cup in Indian Wells, California. After beating Steffi Graf in the finals, 6-3, 3-6, 7-5, her world ranking improved to number 16.

The next big match for Serena was the finals of the 1999 Lipton Championship, where she faced her sister Venus for the title. This match marked the first time in over 100 years that two sisters had met each other in the singles final of a major professional tennis tournament. The whole tennis world was watching to see what would happen. Richard Williams seemed to enjoy all the excitement. He drove around the tennis tournament complex in a minivan with huge pictures of his daughters' faces on the sides. And when the final match began, he held up a sign from his seat in the stadium that read, "Welcome to the Williams show!"

Williams holds the U.S. Open trophy after her win over Martina Hingis, September 11, 1999. Williams defeated Hingis 6-3, 7-6.

Serena and Venus seemed to feel the pressure, as they made many more errors than usual in the match. In the end, Serena lost to her older sister, 6-1, 4-6, 6-4. But she seemed to take the loss in stride. Although the sisters are very competitive when they step onto the tennis court on opposite sides of the net, they are best friends again as soon as the match is over. "Family comes first, no matter how many times we play each other," Serena explained. "Nothing will come between me and my sister."

The 1999 U.S. Open

Many people anticipated a possible rematch between the Williams sisters at the 1999 U.S. Open. Serena and Venus were placed in opposite sides of the draw, which meant that the only time they would have to play against each other would be if they both reached the finals. But this time, the result would be a Grand Slam title. "Now that would be really exciting because either way, one of us would win our first Grand Slam," Serena said at the time.

As the tournament progressed, both Serena and Venus beat their early round opponents to move closer to the final. But then Venus lost a tough, three-set match to Martina Hingis in the semifinals, just one match away from the big showdown. Although she was disappointed for her sister, Serena managed to hold off Lindsay Davenport, 6-4, 1-6, 6-4, and advance to the final against Hingis. "Venus was so bummed yesterday; I really felt terrible," she recalled. "And that encouraged me to be even tougher out there."

"It was pretty exciting," she said about winning the U.S. Open. "I'm thinking, 'Should I scream? Should I yell? Should I cry? What should I do?' I guess I ended up doing them all."

Thrilled at the prospect of playing in her first Grand Slam final, Serena came out strong against Hingis, who appeared tired from her earlier match with Venus. Williams held on to win the 1999 U.S. Open by a score of 6-3, 7-6. When Hingis's last ball sailed out and Serena realized she had won, she was overcome with joy. "It was pretty exciting," she related. "I'm thinking, 'Should I scream? Should I yell? Should I cry? What should I do?' I guess I ended up doing them all."

At age 17, Serena Williams had become the first African-American to win a Grand Slam tennis singles title since Arthur Ashe won Wimbledon in 1975. She was also the first African-American woman to win the U.S. Open since Althea Gibson in 1958. In addition, she took home a check for $750,000. Shortly after the win, Serena got a telephone call from the President Bill Clinton.

Venus Williams, left, gets a kiss from her puppy as sister Serena Williams looks on after they won the women's doubles at the U.S. Open, September 12, 1999.

"Congratulations. We're proud of you," President Clinton told her. "We were thrilled. I mean, the whole White House was out there cheering for you." The next day, the Williams sisters teamed up to claim the women's doubles title at the U.S. Open.

Working to Be Number One

After winning the U.S. Open title, Serena's world ranking jumped all the way to number four. But she still had goals to accomplish in tennis: to become the number one player in the world, and to beat her sister Venus in a tournament. She got the chance to achieve one of her goals at the 1999

Grand Slam Cup. Once again, the Williams sisters squared off against each other in the finals. Serena had arrived in the finals by defeating Lindsay Davenport in the semifinals, just as she had at the U.S. Open. But this time, Venus won her semifinal match against Martina Hingis.

During the all-Williams final, Serena defeated Venus, 6-1, 3-6, 6-3. Although both women are disappointed whenever they lose, the sisters consistently assert that they continue to be best friends regardless of what happens on the court. "I think people expect us not to get along, but that's practically impossible. I don't see how anything could change," Serena noted. "Tennis is a game; it's not your life. We really believe in family."

By the end of the 1999 season, Serena Williams had established herself as one of the outstanding young talents in women's tennis. However, her playing ability has sometimes been overshadowed by controversy. Her father has occasionally made provocative comments about other players, racial issues, and his daughters' abilities. In addition, some players on the women's tour have criticized the Williams sisters, saying that they are unfriendly. But other players and analysts have come to the sisters' defense, arguing that they are no less approachable than other

Serena and Venus Williams are very aware that their success and fame give them a chance to be role models and encourage more African-Americans to enter the white-dominated world of tennis. "Let's face it, there are not many black people in [this] sport," Serena stated. "Black people are definitely going to look at me and say I want to be like her. But a lot of other people do that too."

teenage stars like Martina Hingis or Anna Kournikova. These supporters attribute the criticism to underlying racism in the predominantly white sport of tennis. According to Bart McGuire, chief executive officer of the WTA Tour, "The Williams sisters are a huge plus for the tour off the court as well as on."

HOME AND FAMILY

Serena Williams, who is not married, has lived with her parents on a ten-acre homestead in Florida for many years. At this home, she has her own tennis courts to practice on. Now that she is getting older, however, she is preparing to be on her own. She and her sister Venus have purchased a

Serena Williams, right, and her sister Venus hold their trophies following the women's final at the Grand Slam Cup in Munich, October 3, 1999.

piece of land not far from their family's home. They plan to build a mansion there and move in together.

All of the Williamses, except for father Richard, are Jehovah's Witnesses. Part of their religion involves talking to other people about their beliefs and trying to convert them. Their mother has taken them door-to-door to share their beliefs since they were small children. Serena and Venus also give religious literature to fellow players whenever they can. "I'm not aware of any I've converted, "Serena admitted. "People slam doors on us but that's their problem. We don't take it personally."

HOBBIES AND OTHER INTERESTS

Williams has a wide variety of interests outside of tennis. She likes to surf, ride jet skis, go in-line skating, play the guitar, ride dirt bikes, and drive her BMW to the mall and go shopping. She is also learning to speak Portuguese, and she already knows French. In fact, when she won a title in Paris, she was able to give part of her victory speech in French. Along with her sister Venus, Serena publishes a tennis newsletter called *The Tennis Monthly Recap*. The newsletter includes interesting stories from the world of tennis and interviews with famous tennis players.

Serena's success on the tennis court has led to a number of endorsement opportunities. She signed a multi-million dollar contract with Puma and wears their clothing. She also provides her ideas on clothing styles and new outfit designs. She likes to get away from the traditional tennis whites and wear brightly colored outfits. She also adds color to her look by wearing beads in her braided hair. It takes her mother several hours to braid her hair and string approximately 2000 beads in her braids. The beads and the new-look clothes have became the Williams sisters' trademarks.

Serena and Venus Williams use their fame to inspire other people to play tennis and to help raise money for children's charities. They teach at tennis clinics for inner-city children and they participate in programs that provide tennis-playing opportunities to children who would not otherwise have the chance. They are very aware that their success and fame give them a chance to be role models and encourage more African-Americans to enter the white-dominated world of tennis. "Let's face it, there are not many black people in [this] sport," Serena stated. "Black people are definitely going to look at me and say I want to be like her. But a lot of other people do that too."

HONORS AND AWARDS

European, Women's Doubles: 1998
IGA Classic, Women's Doubles: 1998
U.S. Open, Mixed Doubles: 1998
Wimbledon, Mixed Doubles: 1998
Acura Classic, Women's Singles: 1999
Evert Cup, Women's Singles: 1999
Grand Slam Cup, Women's Singles: 1999
Hanover, Women's Doubles: 1999
French Open, Women's Doubles: 1999
Paris Open, Women's Singles: 1999
U.S. Open, Women's Singles: 1999
U.S. Open, Women's Doubles: 1999
Faber Grand Prix, Women's Singles: 2000

FURTHER READING

BOOKS

Fillon, Mike. *Superstars of Tennis: The Venus and Serena Williams Story,* 1999 (juvenile)
Flynn, Gabriel. *Venus and Serena Williams,* 1999 (juvenile)

Stewart, Mark. *Venus and Serena Williams: Sisters in Arms,* 2000 (juvenile)
Who's Who in America, 2000

Periodicals

Current Biography 1998
Essence, Dec. 1999, p.68
Jet, Dec. 1, 1997, p.48; Sep. 27, 1999, p.51
New York Post, Jan. 23, 2000, p.78
New York Times Magazine, Mar. 16, 1997, p.28
Newsweek, Aug. 25, 1998, p.44
People, Sep. 27, 1999, p.68
Seventeen, July 1998, p.60
Sport, July 1998, p.70
Sports Illustrated, Mar. 22, 1999, p.18; Apr. 5, 1999, p.68; May 31, 1999,
    p.88; Sep. 20, 1999, p.38
Sports Illustrated for Kids, Aug. 1998, p.34
Tennis, Sep. 1998, p.65; Nov. 1999, p.36
Time, Sep. 20, 1999, p.58
USA Today, Mar. 22, 1999, p.C3; Jan. 21, 2000, p.C9; Feb. 18, 2000, p.C4
Washington Post, Sep. 3, 1999, p.D1
Women's Sports and Fitness, Nov./Dec. 1998, p.102

ADDRESS

Corel WTA Tour
1266 E. Main St., 4th Floor
Stamford, CT 06902-5346

WORLD WIDE WEB SITE

http://www.corelwtatour.com

Photo and Illustration Credits

Wilt Chamberlain/Photos: Robert Beck/Sports Illustrated; copyright © Bettmann/CORBIS; AP/Wide World Photos.

Brandi Chastain/Photos: copyright © Reuters Newmedia Inc./CORBIS; AP/Wide World Photos; copyright © AFP/CORBIS; AP/Wide World Photos.

Derek Jeter/Photos: AP/Wide World Photos.

Karch Kiraly/Photos: Peter Brouillet; John McDonough/*Sports Illustrated*; AP/Wide World Photos. Cover: Cover design by James Tran and Lisa-Theresa Lenthall. Photo of sand by Lou Gaines. Cover photo courtesy of Peter Brouillet.

Alex Lowe/Photos: Andrew Eccles/CORBIS Outline; AP/Wide World Photos.

Randy Moss/Photos: AP/Wide World Photos

Dawn Riley/Photos: Daniel Forster; Tom Zinn; AP/Wide World Photos.

Se Ri Pak/Photos: copyright © LPGA 2000; Pete Fontaine; Jack Stohlman.

Karen Smyers/Photos: copyright © Casey B. Gibson 1999; AP/Wide World Photos.

Kurt Warner/Photos: copyright © 1999 by St. Louis Rams; AP/Wide World Photos.

Serena Williams/Photos: copyright © Reuters Newmedia Inc./CORBIS; AP/Wide World Photos; copyright © AFP/CORBIS; copyright © Reuters Newmedia Inc./CORBIS; copyright © AFP/CORBIS.

How to Use the
Cumulative Index

Our indexes have a new look. In an effort to make our indexes easier to use, we've combined the Name and General Index into a new, cumulative General Index. This single ready-reference resource covers all the volumes in *Biography Today*, both the general series and the special subject series. The new General Index contains complete listings of all individuals who have appeared in *Biography Today* since the series began. Their names appear in bold-faced type, followed by the issue in which they appear. The General Index also includes references for the occupations, nationalities, and ethnic and minority origins of individuals profiled in *Biography Today*.

We have also made some changes to our specialty indexes, the Places of Birth Index and the Birthday Index. To consolidate and to save space, the Places of Birth Index and the Birthday Index will no longer appear in the January and April issues of the softbound subscription series. But these indexes can still be found in the September issue of the softbound subscription series, in the hardbound Annual Cumulation at the end of each year, and in each volume of the special subject series.

General Series

The General Series of *Biography Today* is denoted in the index with the month and year of the issue in which the individual appeared. Each individual also appears in the Annual Cumulation for that year.

Special Subject Series

The Special Subject Series of *Biography Today* are each denoted in the index with an abbreviated form of the series name, plus the number of the volume in which the individual appears. They are listed as follows.

Adams, Ansel	Artist V.1	(Artists Series)
Danzinger, Paula	Author V.6	(Authors Series)
Harris, Bernard	Science V.3	(Scientists & Inventors Series)
Lobo, Rebecca	Sport V.3	(Sports Series)
Peterson, Roger Tory	WorLdr V.1	(World Leaders Series: Environmental Leaders)
Sadat, Anwar	WorLdr V.2	(World Leaders Series: Modern African Leaders)
Wolf, Hazel	WorLdr V.3	(World Leaders Series: Environmental Leaders 2)

Updates

Updated information on selected individuals appears in the Appendix at the end of the *Biography Today* Annual Cumulation. In the index, the original entry is listed first, followed by any updates.

Arafat, Yasir . . Sep 94; Update 94; Update 95; Update 96; Update 97; Update 98

Gates, Bill . . . . Apr 93; Update 98

Griffith Joyner, Florence . . . . Sport V.1; Update 98

Sanders, Barry . . . . Sep 95; Update 99

Spock, Dr. Benjamin . . . . Sep 95; Update 98

Yeltsin, Boris . . . . Apr 92; Update 93; Update 95; Update 96; Update 98

General Index

This index includes names, occupations, nationalities, and ethnic and minority origins that pertain to individuals profiled in *Biography Today*.

Places of Birth Index

The following index lists the places of birth for the individuals profiled in *Biography Today*. Places of birth are entered under state, province, and/or country.

Birthday Index

Biography Today

General Series

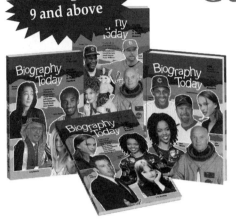

Biography Today **General Series** includes a unique combination of current biographical profiles that teachers and librarians — and the readers themselves — tell us are most appealing. The **General Series** is available as a 3-issue subscription; hardcover annual cumulation; or subscription plus cumulation.

Within the **General Series**, your readers will find a variety of sketches about:

- Authors
- Musicians
- Political leaders
- Sports figures
- Movie actresses & actors
- Cartoonists
- Scientists
- Astronauts
- TV personalities
- and the movers & shakers in many other fields!

"*Biography Today* will be useful in elementary and middle school libraries and in public library children's collections where there is a need for biographies of current personalities. High schools serving reluctant readers may also want to consider a subscription."
— *Booklist,* American Library Association

"Highly recommended for the young adult audience. Readers will delight in the accessible, energetic, tell-all style; teachers, librarians, and parents will welcome the clever format, intelligent and informative text. It should prove especially useful in motivating "reluctant" readers or literate nonreaders."
— *MultiCultural Review*

"Written in a friendly, almost chatty tone, the profiles offer quick, objective information. While coverage of current figures makes *Biography Today* a useful reference tool, an appealing format and wide scope make it a fun resource to browse." — *School Library Journal*

"The best source for current information at a level kids can understand."
— Kelly Bryant, School Librarian, Carlton, OR

"Easy for kids to read. We love it! Don't want to be without it."
— Lynn McWhirter, School Librarian, Rockford, IL

ONE-YEAR SUBSCRIPTION
- 3 softcover issues, 6" x 9"
- Published in January, April, and September
- 1-year subscription, $56
- 150 pages per issue
- 10-12 profiles per issue
- Contact sources for additional information
- Cumulative General, Places of Birth, and Birthday Indexes

HARDBOUND ANNUAL CUMULATION
- Sturdy 6" x 9" hardbound volume
- Published in December
- $57 per volume
- 450 pages per volume
- 30-36 profiles — includes all profiles found in softcover issues for that calendar year
- Cumulative General, Places of Birth, and Birthday Indexes
- Special appendix features current updates of previous profiles

SUBSCRIPTION AND CUMULATION COMBINATION
- $99 for 3 softcover issues plus the hardbound volume

1992

Paula Abdul
Andre Agassi
Kirstie Alley
Terry Anderson
Roseanne Arnold
Isaac Asimov
James Baker
Charles Barkley
Larry Bird
Judy Blume
Berke Breathed
Garth Brooks
Barbara Bush
George Bush
Fidel Castro
Bill Clinton
Bill Cosby
Diana, Princess of Wales
Shannen Doherty
Elizabeth Dole
David Duke
Gloria Estefan
Mikhail Gorbachev
Steffi Graf
Wayne Gretzky
Matt Groening
Alex Haley
Hammer
Martin Handford
Stephen Hawking
Hulk Hogan
Saddam Hussein
Lee Iacocca
Bo Jackson
Mae Jemison
Peter Jennings
Steven Jobs
Pope John Paul II
Magic Johnson
Michael Jordon
Jackie Joyner-Kersee
Spike Lee
Mario Lemieux
Madeleine L'Engle
Jay Leno
Yo-Yo Ma
Nelson Mandela
Wynton Marsalis
Thurgood Marshall
Ann Martin
Barbara McClintock
Emily Arnold McCully
Antonia Novello
Sandra Day O'Connor
Rosa Parks

Jane Pauley
H. Ross Perot
Luke Perry
Scottie Pippen
Colin Powell
Jason Priestley
Queen Latifah
Yitzhak Rabin
Sally Ride
Pete Rose
Nolan Ryan
H. Norman
  Schwarzkopf
Jerry Seinfeld
Dr. Seuss
Gloria Steinem
Clarence Thomas
Chris Van Allsburg
Cynthia Voigt
Bill Watterson
Robin Williams
Oprah Winfrey
Kristi Yamaguchi
Boris Yeltsin

1993

Maya Angelou
Arthur Ashe
Avi
Kathleen Battle
Candice Bergen
Boutros Boutros-Ghali
Chris Burke
Dana Carvey
Cesar Chavez
Henry Cisneros
Hillary Rodham Clinton
Jacques Cousteau
Cindy Crawford
Macaulay Culkin
Lois Duncan
Marian Wright Edelman
Cecil Fielder
Bill Gates
Sara Gilbert
Dizzy Gillespie
Al Gore
Cathy Guisewite
Jasmine Guy
Anita Hill
Ice-T
Darci Kistler
k.d. lang
Dan Marino
Rigoberta Menchu
Walter Dean Myers

Martina Navratilova
Phyllis Reynolds Naylor
Rudolf Nureyev
Shaquille O'Neal
Janet Reno
Jerry Rice
Mary Robinson
Winona Ryder
Jerry Spinelli
Denzel Washington
Keenen Ivory Wayans
Dave Winfield

1994

Tim Allen
Marian Anderson
Mario Andretti
Ned Andrews
Yasir Arafat
Bruce Babbitt
Mayim Bialik
Bonnie Blair
Ed Bradley
John Candy
Mary Chapin Carpenter
Benjamin Chavis
Connie Chung
Beverly Cleary
Kurt Cobain
F.W. de Klerk
Rita Dove
Linda Ellerbee
Sergei Fedorov
Zlata Filipovic
Daisy Fuentes
Ruth Bader Ginsburg
Whoopi Goldberg
Tonya Harding
Melissa Joan Hart
Geoff Hooper
Whitney Houston
Dan Jansen
Nancy Kerrigan
Alexi Lalas
Charlotte Lopez
Wilma Mankiller
Shannon Miller
Toni Morrison
Richard Nixon
Greg Norman
Severo Ochoa
River Phoenix
Elizabeth Pine
Jonas Salk
Richard Scarry
Emmitt Smith

Will Smith
Steven Spielberg
Patrick Stewart
R.L. Stine
Lewis Thomas
Barbara Walters
Charlie Ward
Steve Young
Kim Zmeskal

1995

Troy Aikman
Jean-Bertrand Aristide
Oksana Baiul
Halle Berry
Benazir Bhutto
Jonathan Brandis
Warren E. Burger
Ken Burns
Candace Cameron
Jimmy Carter
Agnes de Mille
Placido Domingo
Janet Evans
Patrick Ewing
Newt Gingrich
John Goodman
Amy Grant
Jesse Jackson
James Earl Jones
Julie Krone
David Letterman
Rush Limbaugh
Heather Locklear
Reba McEntire
Joe Montana
Cosmas Ndeti
Hakeem Olajuwon
Ashley Olsen
Mary-Kate Olsen
Jennifer Parkinson
Linus Pauling
Itzhak Perlman
Cokie Roberts
Wilma Rudolph
Salt 'N' Pepa
Barry Sanders
William Shatner
Elizabeth George
  Speare
Dr. Benjamin Spock
Jonathan Taylor
  Thomas
Vicki Van Meter
Heather Whitestone
Pedro Zamora

1996

Aung San Suu Kyi
Boyz II Men
Brandy
Ron Brown
Mariah Carey
Jim Carrey
Larry Champagne III
Christo
Chelsea Clinton
Coolio
Bob Dole
David Duchovny
Debbie Fields
Chris Galeczka
Jerry Garcia
Jennie Garth
Wendy Guey
Tom Hanks
Alison Hargreaves
Sir Edmund Hillary
Judith Jamison
Barbara Jordan
Annie Leibovitz
Carl Lewis
Jim Lovell
Mickey Mantle
Lynn Margulis
Iqbal Masih
Mark Messier
Larisa Oleynik
Christopher Pike
David Robinson
Dennis Rodman
Selena
Monica Seles
Don Shula
Kerri Strug
Tiffani-Amber Thiessen
Dave Thomas
Jaleel White

1997

Madeleine Albright
Marcus Allen
Gillian Anderson
Rachel Blanchard
Zachery Ty Bryan
Adam Ezra Cohen
Claire Danes
Celine Dion
Jean Driscoll
Louis Farrakhan
Ella Fitzgerald

Harrison Ford
Bryant Gumbel
John Johnson
Michael Johnson
Maya Lin
George Lucas
John Madden
Bill Monroe
Alanis Morissette
Sam Morrison
Rosie O'Donnell
Muammar el-Qaddafi
Christopher Reeve
Pete Sampras
Pat Schroeder
Rebecca Sealfon
Tupac Shakur
Tabitha Soren
Herbert Tarvin
Merlin Tuttle
Mara Wilson

1998

Bella Abzug
Kofi Annan
Neve Campbell
Sean Combs (Puff
   Daddy)
Dalai Lama (Tenzin
   Gyatso)
Diana, Princess of Wales
Leonardo DiCaprio
Walter E. Diemer
Ruth Handler
Hanson
Livan Hernandez
Jewel
Jimmy Johnson
Tara Lipinski
Oseola McCarty
Dominique Moceanu
Alexandra Nechita
Brad Pitt
LeAnn Rimes
Emily Rosa
David Satcher
Betty Shabazz
Kordell Stewart
Shinichi Suzuki
Mother Teresa
Mike Vernon
Reggie White
Venus Williams
Kate Winslet

1999

Ben Affleck
Jennifer Aniston
Maurice Ashley
Kobe Bryant
Bessie Delany
Sadie Delany
Sharon Draper
Sarah Michelle Gellar
John Glenn
Savion Glover
Jeff Gordon
David Hampton
Lauryn Hill
King Hussein
Lynn Johnston
Shari Lewis
Oseola McCarty
Mark McGwire
Slobodan Milosevic
Natalie Portman
J. K. Rowling
Frank Sinatra
Gene Siskel
Sammy Sosa
John Stanford
Natalia Toro
Shania Twain
Mitsuko Uchida
Jesse Ventura
Venus Williams

2000

Christina Aguilera
K.A. Applegate
Backstreet Boys
Daisy Bates
Harry Blackmun
Carson Daly
Ron Dayne
Henry Louis Gates, Jr.
Katie Holmes
Charlayne Hunter-Gault
Johanna Johnson
Craig Kielburger
Ricky Martin
John McCain
Walter Payton
Freddie Prinze, Jr.
Briana Scurry
CeCe Winans

Biography Today
Subject Series

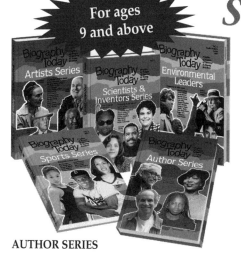

Expands and complements the General Series and targets specific subject areas ...

Our readers asked for it! They wanted more biographies, and the *Biography Today* **Subject Series** is our response to that demand. Now your readers can choose their special areas of interest and go on to read about their favorites in those fields. Priced at just $38 per volume, the following specific volumes are included in the *Biography Today* **Subject Series**:

- **Artists Series**
- **Author Series**
- **Scientists & Inventors Series**
- **Sports Series**
- **World Leaders Series**
  Environmental Leaders
  Modern African Leaders

AUTHOR SERIES

"A useful tool for children's assignment needs." — *School Library Journal*

"The prose is workmanlike: report writers will find enough detail to begin sound investigations, and browsers are likely to find someone of interest." — *School Library Journal*

Scientists & Inventors Series

"The articles are readable, attractively laid out, and touch on important points that will suit assignment needs. Browsers will note the clear writing and interesting details." — *School Library Journal*

"The book is excellent for demonstrating that scientists are real people with widely diverse backgrounds and personal interests. The biographies are fascinating to read." — *The Science Teacher*

SPORTS SERIES

"This series should become a standard resource in libraries that serve intermediate students." — *School Library Journal*

ENVIRONMENTAL LEADERS #1

"A tremendous book that fills a gap in the biographical category of books. This is a great reference book." — *Science Scope*

FEATURES AND FORMAT

- Sturdy 6" x 9" hardbound volumes
- Individual volumes, $39 each
- 200 pages per volume
- 12 profiles per volume — targets individuals within a specific subject area
- Contact sources for additional information
- Cumulative General, Places of Birth, and Birthday Indexes

NOTE: There is *no duplication of entries* between the **General Series** of *Biography Today* and the **Subject Series**.

Artists Series

VOLUME 1

Ansel Adams
Romare Bearden
Margaret Bourke-White
Alexander Calder
Marc Chagall
Helen Frankenthaler
Jasper Johns
Jacob Lawrence
Henry Moore
Grandma Moses
Louise Nevelson
Georgia O'Keeffe
Gordon Parks
I.M. Pei
Diego Rivera
NormanRockwell
Andy Warhol
Frank Lloyd Wright

Author Series

VOLUME 1

Eric Carle
Alice Childress
Robert Cormier
Roald Dahl
Jim Davis
John Grisham
Virginia Hamilton
James Herriot
S.E. Hinton
M.E. Kerr
Stephen King
Gary Larson
Joan Lowery Nixon
Gary Paulsen
Cynthia Rylant
Mildred D. Taylor
Kurt Vonnegut, Jr.
E.B. White
Paul Zindel

VOLUME 2

James Baldwin
Stan and Jan Berenstain
David Macaulay
Patricia MacLachlan
Scott O'Dell
Jerry Pinkney
Jack Prelutsky
Lynn Reid Banks
Faith Ringgold
J.D. Salinger
Charles Schulz
Maurice Sendak
P.L. Travers
Garth Williams

VOLUME 3

Candy Dawson Boyd
Ray Bradbury
Gwendolyn Brooks
Ralph Ellison
Louise Fitzhugh
Jean Craighead George
E.L. Konigsburg
C.S. Lewis
Fredrick McKissack
Patricia McKissack
Katherine Paterson
Anne Rice
Shel Silverstein
Laura Ingalls Wilder

VOLUME 4

Betsy Byars
Chris Carter
Caroline Cooney
Christopher Paul Curtis
Anne Frank
Robert Heinlein
Marguerite Henry
Melissa Mathison
Bill Peet
Lois Lowry
August Wilson

VOLUME 5

Sharon Creech
Michael Crichton
Karen Cushman
Tomie de Paola
Lorraine Hansberry
Karen Hesse
Brian Jacques
Gary Soto
Richard Wright
Laurence Yep

VOLUME 6

Lloyd Alexander
Paula Danziger
Nancy Farmer
Zora Neale Hurston
Shirley Jackson
Angela Johnson
Jon Krakauer
Leo Lionni
Francine Pascal
Louis Sachar
Kevin Williamson

VOLUME 7

William H. Armstrong
Patricia Reilly Giff
Langston Hughes
Stan Lee
Julius Lester
Robert Pinsky
Todd Strasser
Jacqueline Woodson
Patricia C. Wrede
Jane Yolen

VOLUME 8

Barbara Cooney
Chris Crutcher
Paul Lawrence Dunbar
Ursula K. LeGuin
Terry McMillan
Farley Mowat
Naomi Shahoub Nye
Daniel Pinkwater
Beatrix Potter
Ann Rinaldi

Scientists & Inventors Series

VOLUME 1

John Bardeen
Sylvia Earle
Dian Fossey
Jane Goodall
Bernadine Healy
Jack Horner
Mathilde Krim
Edwin Land
Louise & Mary Leakey
Rita Levi-Montalcini
J. Robert Oppenheimer
Albert Sabin
Carl Sagan
James D. Watson

VOLUME 2

Jane Brody
Seymour Cray
Paul Erdös
Walter Gilbert
Stephen Jay Gould
Shirley Ann Jackson
Raymond Kurzweil
Shannon Lucid
Margaret Mead
Garrett Morgan
Bill Nye
Eloy Rodriguez
An Wang

VOLUME 3

Luis Alvarez
Hans A. Bethe
Gro Harlem Brundtland
Mary S. Calderone
Ioana Dumitriu
Temple Grandin
John L. Gwaltney
Bernard Harris
Jerome H. Lemelson
Susan Love
Ruth Patrick
Oliver Sacks
Richie Stachowski

Sports Series

VOLUME 1

Hank Aaron
Kareem Abdul-Jabbar
Hassiba Boulmerka
Susan Butcher
Beth Daniel
Chris Evert
Ken Griffey, Jr.
Florence Griffith Joyner
Grant Hill
Greg Lemond
Pelé
Uta Pippig
Cal Ripken, Jr.
Arantxa Sanchez Vicario
Deion Sanders
Tiger Woods

VOLUME 2

Muhammad Ali
Donovan Bailey
Gail Devers
John Elway
Brett Favre
Mia Hamm
Anfernee "Penny" Hardaway
Martina Hingis
Gordie Howe
Jack Nicklaus
Richard Petty
Dot Richardson
Sheryl Swoopes
Steve Yzerman

VOLUME 3

Joe Dumars
Jim Harbaugh
Dominik Hasek
Michelle Kwan
Rebecca Lobo
Greg Maddux
Fatuma Roba
Jackie Robinson
John Stockton
Picabo Street
Pat Summitt
Amy Van Dyken

VOLUME 4

Wilt Chamberlain
Brandi Chastain
Derek Jeter
Karch Kiraly
Alex Lowe
Randy Moss
Se RiPak
Dawn Riley
Karen Smyers
Kurt Warner
Serena Williams

World Leaders Series

VOLUME 1: Environmental Leaders 1

Edward Abbey
Renee Askins
David Brower
Rachel Carson
Marjory Stoneman Douglas
Dave Foreman
Lois Gibbs
Wangari Maathai
Chico Mendes
Russell Mittermeier
Margaret and Olaus Murie
Patsy Ruth Oliver
Roger Tory Peterson
Ken Saro-Wiwa
Paul Watson
Adam Werbach

VOLUME 2: Modern African Leaders

Mohammed Farah Aidid
Idi Amin
Hastings Kamuzu Banda
Haile Selassie
Hassan II
Kenneth Kaunda
Jomo Kenyatta
Mobutu Sese Seko
Robert Mugabe
Kwame Nkrumah
Winnie Mandela
Julius Kambarage Nyerere
Anwar Sadat
Jonas Savimbi
Léopold Sédar Senghor
William V. S. Tubman

VOLUME 3: Environmental Leaders 2

John Cronin
Dai Qing
Ka Hsaw Wa
Winona LaDuke
Aldo Leopold
Bernard Martin
Cynthia Moss
John Muir
Gaylord Nelson
Douglas Tompkins
Hazel Wolf

biography for beginners

"Useful in elementary-school library media centers and public libraries."
— *Booklist,* American Library Association

"Great for reluctant readers."
— M. Younger, Librarian, Caledonia, MI

"Well-thought-out and beautifully, masterfully presented."
— Mary Lynne Rowe, School Librarian, Adel, GA

"The books arrived just as our fourth grade classes were doing biographical reports, and the books contained just the material they needed."
— Carrol Grabill, Media Specialist, Wyoming, MI

We like biographies too! Created especially for your youngest readers (ages 6-9), *Biography for Beginners* includes facts and information about:

- Authors
- Artists & cartoonists
- TV & film stars
- Musicians
- Scientists
- Sports stars
- World figures

Type size, page size, sentence length, and vocabulary have all been chosen for the lower-elementary-grade reader. Pronunciations for unfamiliar words and definitions of terms are also included.

FEATURES AND FORMAT

- Sturdy 7" x 10" hardbound issues
- 2 issues per year (Spring and Fall)
- Just $40 for both issues
- 100 pages per issue
- 10-15 entries per issue
- Contact sources for additional information
- Easy-to-use cumulative Name, Subject, and Birthday Indexes

Biography for Beginners: Presidents of the United States

Now young readers ages 7-10 have a lively, informative, and illustrated biographical source covering all of the Presidents of the United States, from George Washington to Bill Clinton. Biographical information is presented in a format and writing style similar to the popular *Biography for Beginners* series.

MAJOR FEATURES

- Sturdy 8½" x 11" hardbound volume
- Priced at $50
- 467 pages
- 41 entries
- Heavily illustrated
- Includes quotes and short anecdotes
- Contact sources for additional information
- Easy-to-use Subject Index
- Features three appendices
- Glossary of political and presidential terms

"A solid introduction to America's leaders for beginning researchers." — *School Library Journal*

1995

Jan Berenstain
Stan Berenstain
Bonnie Blair
Judy Blume
Jan Brett
Eric Carle
Beverly Cleary
Bill Clinton
Joanna Cole
Jim Davis
Ken Griffey, Jr.
Melissa Joan Hart
Jackie Joyner-Kersee
Ezra Jack Keats
Nancy Kerrigan
Arnold Lobel
Nelson Mandela
Shannon Miller
Joe Montana
Ashley Olsen
Mary-Kate Olsen
Shaquille O'Neal
Rosa Parks
Jack Prelutsky
Richard Scarry
Jon Scieszka
Dr. Seuss
Emmitt Smith
Jonathan Taylor Thomas

1996

Aliki
Tim Allen
Brandy
Chelsea Clinton
Hillary Clinton
Gloria Estefan
Jane Goodall
Wayne Gretzky
Jim Henson
Mae Jemison
Yo-Yo Ma
Ann M. Martin
Hakeem Olajuwon
Larisa Oleynik
Colin Powell
Cal Ripken, Jr.
David Robinson
Cynthia Rylant
Charles Schulz
Maurice Sendak

Chris Van Allsburg
Rosemary Wells
Laura Ingalls Wilder
Garth Williams

1997

Zachery Ty Bryan
Virginia Lee Burton
Matt Christopher
Al Gore
Grant Hill
Jack Horner
Michael Jordan
Shannon Lucid
James Marshall
Mercer Mayer
Peggy Parish
Bill Peet
Pele
Patricia Polacco
Shel Silverstein
Kerri Strug
Dave Thomas
Jaleel White
Mara Wilson
Kristi Yamaguchi

1998

Marc Brown
LeVar Burton
Janell Cannon
Tomie dePaola
Mia Hamm
Kevin Henkes
Russell Hoban
Whitney Houston
Tara Lipinski
Fredrick McKissack
Patricia McKissack
Dominique Moceanu
Garrett Morgan
Barbara Park
Itzhak Perlman
Dav Pilkey
Beatrix Potter
Fred Rogers
Mother Teresa
Tiger Woods

1999

Norman Bridwell
Kobe Bryant
Janell Cannon
Donald Crews
Sylvia Earle
Virginia Hamilton
Shari Lewis
Leo Lionni
Jake Lloyd
Wynton Marsalis
Mark McGwire
Laura Numeroff
Bill Nye
Rosie O'Donnell
Faith Ringgold
Briana Scurry
Sammy Sosa
Jane Yolen

2000

K.A. Applegate
Christopher Paul Curtis
Jeff Gordon
Alexandra Nechita
Daniel Pinkwater
David Satcher
William Steig
Sheryl Swoopes
Amy Van Dyken